# THE COMPLETE BOOK OF
# FLOORCLOTHS

# THE COMPLETE BOOK OF
# FLOORCLOTHS

## DESIGNS & TECHNIQUES FOR PAINTING
## GREAT-LOOKING CANVAS RUGS

KATHY COOPER & JAN HERSEY

Lark Books

Asheville, North Carolina

Editor: Leslie Dierks
Art Director: Kathleen Holmes
Illustrations: Kathy Cooper
Production: Elaine Thompson, Kathleen Holmes, Bobby Gold

**Library of Congress Cataloging in Publication Data**
Cooper, Kathy.
    The complete book of floorcloths : designs & techniques for
painting great-looking canvas rugs / Kathy Cooper & Jan Hersey.
        p.   cm.
    Includes index.
    ISBN 1-887374-19-1
    1. Painting.   2. Floor coverings.   I. Hersey, Jan.   II. Title.
TT 385.C67   1997
746.6--DC20                                    96-41383
                                               CIP

10 9 8 7 6 5 4

Published by Lark Books
50 College Street
Asheville, North Carolina 28801

© 1997 by Kathy Cooper and Jan Hersey

Distributed by Random House, Inc., in the United States, Canada,
    the United Kingdom, Europe, and Asia

Distributed in Australia by Capricorn Link (Australia) Pty Ltd., P.O.
    Box 6651, Baulkam Hills Business Centre, NSW 2153, Australia

Distributed in New Zealand by Tandem Press Ltd., 2 Rugby Rd.,
    Birkenhead, Auckland, New Zealand

Unless otherwise indicated, the photography is done by the artist whose
work is depicted. All how-to photography is by Evan Bracken.

*Printed in Hong Kong by Oceanic Graphic Printing Productions Ltd.*

Opposite page, top to
bottom, details of: Maureen
O'Donnell, *Carwitham #2*,
(photograph by David Egan);
Tara Loughlin, *Oranges*,
(photograph by Kevin Brusie);
Mary Moross, *Circus*, (photo-
graph by Ileona Saurez);
Joan Weissman, *Untitled*,
(photograph by Damian
Andrus); Constance Miller,
*The Four Directions*; Gary
Mackender, *Untitled*

# CONTENTS

Top left: George Shinn, *Gold Dust*, 52" x 52" (1.3 x 1.3 m),
stenciled mirror-image repeat acrylics
Photograph: Photocraft Lab

Top right: Kiki Farish and Carol Massenburg, *Bee Balm &
Butterflies*, 2' x 3' (61 x 91.5 cm), stenciled and glazed acrylics
Photograph: J. W. Photo Labs

Bottom: Shari Cornish, *Recognize Anybody?*, 34" x 60"
(.9 x 1.5 m), silk-screened fabric pigment on industrial felt
Photograph: B. Miller

# INTRODUCTION

To contemporary decorators, the floorcloth is a fashionable alternative to area rugs, a way to splash color and design across a living space. Historians, on the other hand, are apt to view painted canvas as a poor man's carpet, used during this country's early years as an inexpensive yet practical floor covering.

Having evolved from a handcraft of the 1700s to a manufactured product of the 1800s, then abandoned in favor of linoleum at the turn of the century, today floorcloths have come full circle: Once again they're the province of individual artists, blending the best of their legacy of craftsmanship with the design, materials, and production techniques of contemporary society.

Most of today's floorcloth makers are self taught. Some use methods similar to those employed in previous centuries, while others prefer modern materials that offer design options our predecessors did not enjoy. Many approaches produce satisfactory results, though the ease of application and resulting rug characteristics may vary.

All floorcloths—a word we use interchangeably with the term *rugs* throughout the book—

are made by laying down on canvas coats of primer, paint, and sealer, one on top of the other. To be durable and age well, these layers must be compatible. For this reason, in this book we have designated the use of contemporary, water-based products. (We have, however, sought to explain the characteristics of these as well as alternative materials in order to provide as much insight as possible into the painting process.) Not only are water-based primers, paints, and

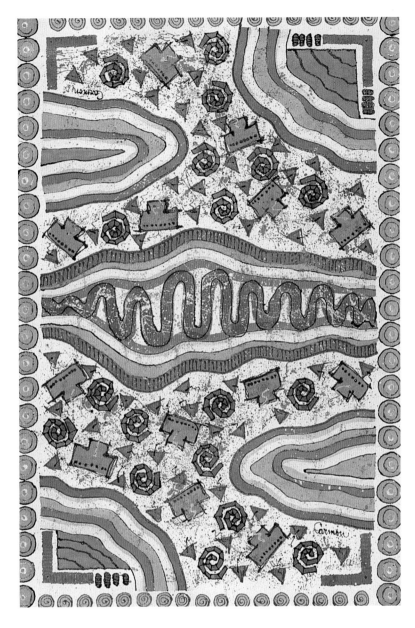

Carmon Slater, *Napoli*, 39" x 57" (1 x 1.4 m), applied pigments
Photograph: Pete Krumhardt

sealers easy to use and clean up, they are also chemically similar and, over the long run, will react at the same rate to the forces of use and nature. Use of these products will thus avert the problems of cracking and crazing, which result from incompatible materials reacting at different rates.

The book is divided into sections to capture your interest, no matter what level of expertise and inspiration you bring to it. If you're new to the medium, the surest road to success is to explore the discussions of planning and materials, then follow the step-by-step instructions for the sample checkered rug in chapter 3. If you have a modest level of painting experience or are comfortable exploring the paint medium, try combining some of the illustrated techniques from chapter 5 with one of the projects in chapter 6. For the adventurous, the discussion of design considerations in chapter 4 and the many colorful photographs of contemporary rugs throughout the book should provide plenty of inspiration to produce your own custom-designed rug.

We hope this book will open a door into a new and visually exciting medium. We invite you to step through and explore this world of contemporary art, creativity, and practical home accessories.

Top: Laura Curran, *Mahjong*, 2' x 3' (61 x 91.5 cm), hand-painted acrylics

Center: Joan Weissman, *Untitled*, 4' x 6' (1.2 x 1.8 m), hand-painted latex
Photograph: Damian Andrus

Right: Jan Harris, *Red Birds & Malachite*, 43" x 64" (1.1 x 1.6 m), woodgrained and stenciled with gold leaf, oils, and acrylics
Photograph: Evan Bracken

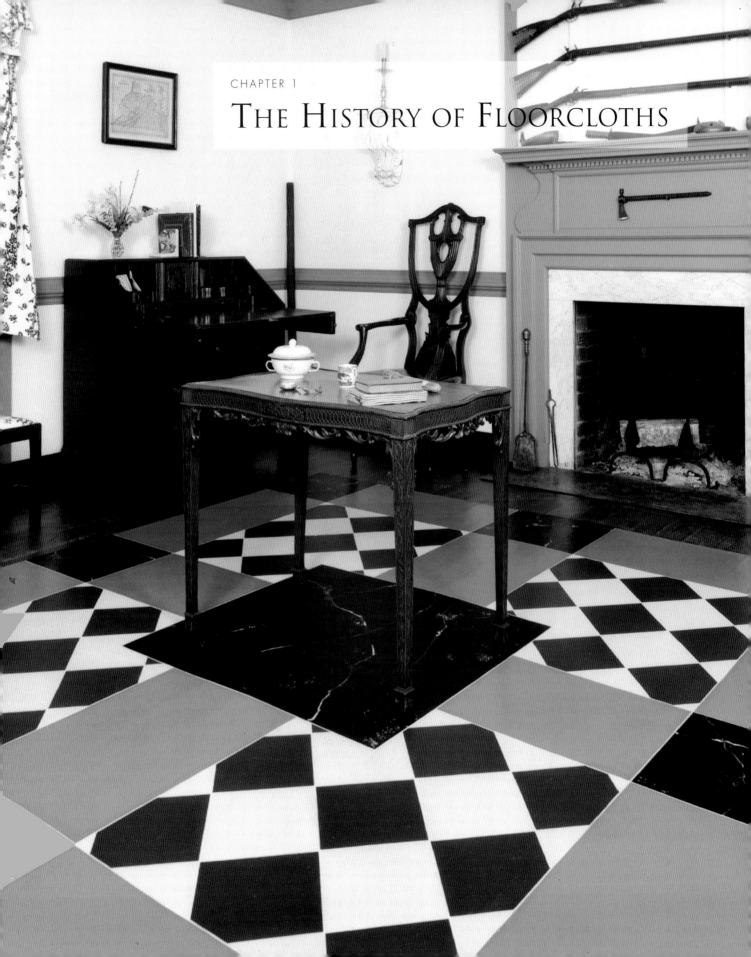

# CHAPTER 1

# THE HISTORY OF FLOORCLOTHS

Previous page: Stuart Bailey,
*Carwitham #12* (1739 English
floorcloth pattern), 6' x 9' (1.8 x
2.7 m), marbled oils
Photograph: Katherine Wetzel

Top left: Thomas Stocker,
*Qashqa'i Tree of Life*, 48" x
79" (1.2 x 2 m), hand-painted
and stenciled acrylics
Photograph: Eric Davis

Top right: Laura Gardner and
Mary Moross, *Fiori*, 4' x 6'
(1.2 x 1.8 m), combed and
hand-painted latex and acrylics
Photograph: Gerin Choinere

Right: Laura Gardner and Mary
Moross, *Black Moon and Stars*,
3' x 6' (.9 x 1.8 m), hand-
painted, stippled, sponged,
and stenciled latex and acrylics
Photograph: Gerin Choinere

PAINTED CANVAS RUGS have their technical roots in stenciled or block-printed cloth game boards, playing cards, religious prints, and table covers of the 1400s; but until the 1700s, textiles were considered too precious to be used on floors.

Most floors in early American and European homes consisted of either tamped earth or unvarnished wood and were generally left bare. If enhanced at all, they were covered with rushes, straw, or sand, which was swept with a broom into swirl, herringbone, or other patterns. Only in the finest homes were floor coverings found, and rarely until the 1700s.

The first written reference to a floorcloth is a 1722 British receipt showing that Benjamin Powell paid "for a Bed Tent and Markee as per receipt £38 8s and for a floor oyled cloth to lye in the tent." Though Powell apparently intended to use his "oyl cloth" as a ground cover in a tent, the fact that he calls it a "floor" oyled cloth indicates that coated fabrics were already in use as floor coverings.

In the 18th century, "floorcloth" was a generic term that referred to a carpet substitute of either treated or untreated wool, linen (flax), or cotton. Floorcloths went by many names: painted, printed, stamped, or common carpet, oil floor cloth, wax cloth, fancy-pattern cloth, Masonic flooring, summer floor mat, and various combinations of the above. By the middle of the 19th century, floorcloths were generally referred to as "oil cloths."

In addition to serving as primary floor coverings, floorcloths also were used as druggets or crumb cloths—thin painted or plain cloths that were laid under a table or sideboard on top of finer carpets or flooring to protect them from spills.

Top: Maureen O'Donnell, detail, *Stars*, full size is 2' x 3' (61 x 91.5 cm), stenciled oils.
Photograph: David Egan

Left: Alexander F. Fraser, ca. 1830-42, *Asking a Blessing*, oil on canvas, 14½ " x 20¼" (36 x 51 cm). In this family scene, an unpainted floorcloth is used as a drugget or crumb cloth beneath the table to protect the large patterned carpet underneath.
Courtesy of Milwaukee Public Museum

11

with both delight and disappointment. *Bulletin 250: Contributions from the Museum of History and Technology* cites a letter from Thomas Nelson, Jr., of Virginia, to Messrs. John Norton and Son, in London in 1773, in which he writes:

> Gentle. Capt. Robertson delivered your Letter of the 29th May enclosing a Bill of Loading for the floor Cloth and Anchovies. The Cloth is injur'd by being role'd before the paint was dry; the Anchovies are very fine, for which Mrs. Nelson returns you her particular thanks.

Some purchasers sought to avert disappointment by requesting that their imported floorcloths be shipped on "rowlers" or that a woolen blanket be rolled between the layers to prevent the paint from rubbing off.

## GROWING PREFERENCE FOR DOMESTIC GOODS

After the American Revolution, the preference for British goods gave way to a nationalistic support of American-made products. Because they didn't compete with finer English goods, cruder textiles such as rope, bagging, and canvas were among the first textiles to gain a foothold in America. As American society matured and a means of exchange replaced barter, the demand for household products grew, and it didn't take long for domestic floorcloth production to rival that of England. Advertisements for locally-made floorcloths (as well as for floor-

## IMPORTED RUGS FOR THE WELL-TO-DO

Until 1720, town commerce in America revolved around shipping and imports; only the rudiments of manufacturing existed in isolated villages close to the sources of raw materials. For their finer fabrics and goods, Americans relied on Britain, where floorcloth production and use were already well established.

By the mid-1700s, retail merchandizing had established a foothold in America. Early merchants' advertisements heralded the arrival of British ships bearing floorcloths—"a few neat London-painted floorcloths, Just imported in the Ship Mary…" (*South Carolina Gazette and Country Journal*, Charleston, July 7, 1767).

Floorcloths were imported by individuals as well as by merchants. Citizens with goods to trade established credit and purchased British merchandise through agents. Such long-distance orders met

cloth repair and repainting) are found almost as early as those for imports, appearing with increasing frequency after 1750.

Local artisans and itinerant artists were the first Americans to offer to paint floorcloths for their customers in both ready-made and custom designs. These same artists could also be found offering "fancy" painting on signs, coaches, chimney boards, and even ships. To meet the growing demand for their services, artisans advertised for help, taking on workers under an apprentice system similar to that found in England. Apparently there was no lack of skilled labor, with help found among the immigrant population (some of whom already possessed the necessary skills), traveling workers, young boys, and indentured servants.

Domestic floorcloths were promoted at first by claiming they were the equal of imports, but after the Revolution, Americans began to view the fruits of their own labor as superior to those of the British. In a story about a new manufacturing company, Messrs. Freneau & Co., in the *City Gazette and Daily Advertiser* (Charleston, South Carolina) of June 13, 1809, the writer stated:

> I am inclined to believe [Freneau's American-made floorcloths] are equal, if not superior, to the English cloths. This may appear strange; however, one observation will suffice to reconcile — The English cloths are so thick and weighty, that when they are moved from place to place, or are not put down with the greatest care, they crack, the colours flake off, and cannot well be repaired; but, on the contrary, the cloths painted here by Mr. WOLPORD, who is the artist, are so pliant as not to be subject to creasing or a flaking off of the colours, and may be used in three weeks after they are painted.

Bottom left: Mary Moross, *Shyrdak*, 72" x 108" (1.8 x 2.7 m), hand-painted water-based paints
Photograph: Ileona Saurez

Bottom right: Evergreene Painting Studios, *Untitled*, 8' x 12' (2.4 x 3.6 m), hand-painted and stenciled acrylics
Photograph: Michael Imlay

## HOME PRODUCTION

Floorcloth production wasn't a specialized art, and from the beginning was practiced by enterprising homeowners as well as by professionals. In his autobiography, Lyman Beecher, father of the Rev. Henry Ward Beecher, enlightens us about home furnishings and floorcloths in his home town of Southampton, New York, around 1800:

> We had no carpets; there was not a carpet from end to end of the town. All had sanded floors, some of them worn through. Your mother introduced the first carpet. Uncle Lot gave me some money, and I had an itch to spend it. Went to a vendue, and bought a bale of cotton. [Mrs. Beecher] spun it, and had it woven; then she laid it down, sized it, and painted it in oils, with a border all around it, and bunches of roses and other flowers over the centre. She sent to New York for her colors, and ground and mixed them herself. The carpet was nailed down on the garret floor, and she used to go there and paint.

No doubt Mrs. Beecher was among those who—developing the taste and pocketbook for finer household goods—were inspired by a continuing stream of books and magazines in England and America, offering advice on how to create and maintain the good life.

Middle-class interest in home furnishings was furthered during the 1800s by lowered postal

Top: Mary Van Vliet, *Sun*, 44" x 44" (112 x 112 cm), stenciled and glazed acrylics

Center: Barbara Farrell, *Big Bandana*, 6' x 8' (1.8 x 2.4 m), glazed and varnished acrylics and latex
Photograph: Patty Fisher

Bottom: Virginia Kirsch, detail, *Renaissance*, full size is 4' x 6' (1.2 x 1.8 m), block-printed acrylics
Photograph: Tom Erikson

rates and improved transportation, which extended the reach of magazines instructing in taste, fashion, and household advice—and the goods that followed them. One important proponent of floorcloths and design was Rufus Porter, who in 1825 published *A Select Collection of Valuable and Curious Arts and Interesting Experiments* with instructions on how "to Paint in Figures For Carpets Or Borders." In 1872 the first mail-order catalog, Montgomery Ward, brought a huge assortment of goods—including floorcloths of all sizes—within reach of even the most rural areas.

As the century progressed, demand for household goods grew and was fed by technological advances in textile and mass production; floorcloth production moved from the workshop to the factory.

Jean Ebert, *Untitled,* inspired by 18th century Masonic ceremonial floor-cloth, 10' x 12' (3 x 3.6 m), hand-painted oils

Photograph: Museum of Early Southern Decorative Arts

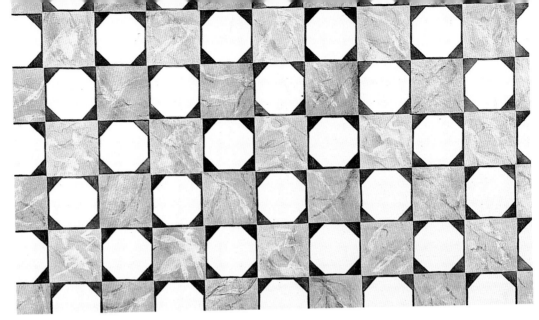

Top: Maureen O'Donnell,
*Carwitham #2* (1700s English
floorcloth pattern), 2' x 3'
(61 x 91.5 cm), marbled,
hand-painted, and stenciled oils
Photograph: David Egan

Bottom left: Maureen
O'Donnell, *Carwitham #4*,
2' x 3' (61 x 91.5 cm), hand-
painted and stenciled oils
Photograph: David Egan

Bottom right: John Carwitham,
*Various Kinds of Floor
Decoration*, plate #2
Courtesy of Library of Congress

2

I. Carwitham Inv. et sc. 1739.

## DESIGNS

From the beginning, floorcloth designs tended to mimic the dominant floors and floor coverings of the day. The earliest cloths were plain or decorated to look like marble, tile, or parquet flooring. The mostly all-over geometric designs included squares, octagons, diamonds, and lozenges, as well as cubes, pyramids, and other three-dimensional effects.

Several books published in England set the design standards followed for many years. Of particular influence were 24 plates published in 1739 by London engraver John Carwitham for *Various Kinds of Floor Decoration Represented in both Plano and Perspective. Being Useful Designs* *for Ornamenting the Floors of Halls &c.... Whether of Stone or Marble, or with Painted Floor Cloths.* Carwitham's striking geometric patterns combined blocks, cubes, and hexagons in a variety of classical looks. Many of the ideas spelled out by him are clearly seen on floor coverings depicted in early American genre paintings, and are still inspiring artists today.

Freehand design was replaced during the 1700s by stenciling, which offered speed, variety, and consistency. Then in 1755, Smith & Baber of London used the first block-printed pattern, said to be a simple one-color design of graduated wavy lines sectioned off into squares. By 1782, Samuel Blythe was

Bottom left: John Carwitham, *Various Kinds of Floor Decoration*, plate #8
Courtesy of Library of Congress

Bottom right: John Carwitham, *Various Kinds of Floor Decoration*, plate #12
Courtesy of Library of Congress

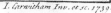

Top: Patricia Dreher,
*Diamonds and Hexagons*,
5' x 9' (1.5 x 2.7 m), hand-
painted, washed, and glazed
acrylics
Photograph: Valerie Massey

Bottom: Stuart Bailey,
*Carwitham #8* (1739 English
floorcloth pattern), 10' x 18'
(3 x 5.5 m), marbled oils
Photograph: Katherine Wetzel

"stamping" carpets in Salem, Massachusetts. Early printing blocks were hardwood with looped leather hand holds. They were pressed onto a cushion of paint and then onto the canvas, where they were tapped with a mallet to ensure a firm impression. The backing for printed carpets was not necessarily primed before painting, though the designs themselves were protected with coats of shellac, which was not always the case with early painted cloths.

By the last quarter of the 18th century, floorcloth designs also imitated Oriental rugs. Flowers, both realistic and stylized, and even animals were appropriate subjects for floorcloth painters. The paintings, portraits, and pattern books of the period point to rich sources of designs.

## COLORS

Like patterns, floorcloth colors followed the trends of the day. And contrary to what we might imagine, colors were not dull. Because of the lack of electric lighting during much of the period when floorcloths were popular, colors were often bright of necessity. Color was a popular topic in contemporary publications, and beginning in 1828, writers were sophisticated enough to advocate the use of analogous and contrasting colors. The development of artificial dyes, beginning in 1850, contributed to brighter, more varied, and more intense hues.

## ENDURING POPULARITY

Floorcloths had much to recommend them to those of both modest and extravagant means and taste. Although they originally were intended to lend the appearance of luxury to those who couldn't afford it, floorcloths came to be accepted and admired on their own merits. Among the reasons given for their appeal were their durability and ease of maintenance: they were not subject to injury from insects, as were wool and straw; in summer they were cool and did not mildew; in winter they kept out drafts and provided an extra layer of protection if used under woven carpets; and they could be reversed, repainted, and repaired.

Floorcloths were used in almost every room of the house, side by side with woven carpets (or sometimes under them or on top of them).

They were particularly useful in those areas subject to dirt and wear, such as entries, hallways, and stairs, both because they were durable and because they could be refurbished or replaced at modest cost should they become worn. They also were used for baths, powdering closets, bedrooms, dressing rooms, and the rooms of "upper" servants. Not limited to floor and home use, painted canvas also found service as table covers and chair bottoms, on carriage or gig floors, and in church pews.

Top: Illustrations of tools used by Joseph Barnes to manufacture floorcloths in England during the 1760s. The drawings were made by Robert Barnes, who included them in an 1857 scrapbook detailing his grandfather's business.
Courtesy of Victoria and Albert Museum, London

Bottom: Many early floorcloth patterns imitated wooden flooring and other types of floor coverings. These fragments, believed to date from the mid- to late-1800s, were found in an attic cistern at the historic Owen Thomas House in Savannah, Georgia. Their designs include paisley, parquet, and "Turkey" (oriental rug) patterns.
Photograph: Museum of Early Southern Decorative Arts

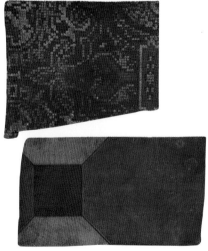

## OVERTAKEN BY TECHNOLOGY

For more than a century, floorcloth production played an important role in the economies of both the United States and Britain. But the same technologies that converged in the second half of the 19th century to make floorcloth manufacture easier and faster than ever also led to its demise. Whereas handcrafted products had striven for function and beauty, manufactured ones boasted convenience; the ideal of mechanical perfection replaced individual artistic expression. Floorcloths were among the many victims of the Industrial Revolution.

In the last quarter of the 19th century, the advent of linoleum—a combination of linseed oil, pulverized cork, gums, and pigments adhered by pressure to a burlap backing— and a growing taste for area rugs finally caused floorcloths to fall from favor. Their last hurrah was in the 1920s, when they were advertised as stove oil cloths for use where ashes and grease could damage other floor coverings.

There is little or no mention of painted canvas after the first quarter of the 20th century, although Armstrong Cork produced similar, felt-based products they called Quaker rugs until the 1960s. Though the medium continued to be used for theater sets, painted canvas rugs were no longer considered a home accessory. For almost a half-century—the one in which today's homeowners have our roots and memories—they were forgotten.

## ROOTS OF THE CONTEMPORARY MOVEMENT

The growing popularity of floorcloths today can be traced to the convergence in the 1950s and 1960s of interest in the authenticity of historic restoration and the concurrent rebirth of a hand-

crafts movement. Rather than simply refurbishing old buildings, historians began furnishing them with appointments appropriate to the home's primary period, and many of America's vintage properties were found to have used floorcloths. A floorcloth for a 1957 restoration of the dining room of the Salem Towne House at Old Sturbridge Village in Sturbridge, Massachusetts, was among the first to reappear.

Sometimes these reproductions were produced by the original methods; others were simply made to look like the originals. Either way, artists began to revive this centuries-old medium, producing first antique designs, then folk and country designs, then branching out to decidedly original and contemporary expressions.

Opposite: Stuart Bailey, *Compass Rose*, 8' x 10' (2.4 x 3 m), marbled oils
Photograph: Katherine Wetzel

Top: Maryellen Murphy, *Hooked Rugs: Twentieth Century Revisited*, 22" x 96" (.5 x 2.4 m), hand-painted acrylics with rug fringe
Photograph: Kate Cameron

Bottom: Patricia Dreher, *Diamonds Light to Dark*, 5' x 8' (1.5 x 2.4 m), hand-painted and glazed acrylics
Photograph: Valerie Massey

Today's floorcloth artists come from many artistic backgrounds, among them weaving and textile design, graphics, print making, crafts, and interior design. They are attracted to floorcloths by their immediacy, artistic freedom, functionality, and a certain irreverence that takes pleasure in making art to be walked upon! Unlike some disciplines that require years of training or expensive tools and materials, the simplicity of this medium affords access to all who wish to explore it.

Floorcloths have grown in popularity as artists discover this uniquely satisfying marriage of art and craft and as the public finds that these practical floor coverings fit into today's trend toward eclectic and practical home decor.

Today floorcloths have moved beyond historic settings into mainstream use. Although the passage of time has had little effect on the method of production of these utilitarian floor coverings—they are still largely made by hand—the historic designs of the past have now been joined by a cornucopia of images and shapes, creating not just floor coverings, but art for the floor.

Top: Wallpaper scrap, Virginia, 18th or early 19th century
Photograph: Museum of Early Southern Decorative Arts

Bottom left: Jean Ebert, *Untitled*, inspired by wallpaper scrap, 5' x 7' (1.5 x 2.1 m), hand-painted and stenciled acrylics
Photograph: Brad Rauschenberg

Bottom right: Pomonoa Shea, *Abstract*, 64" x 100" (1.6 x 2.5 m), hand-painted acrylics
Photograph: Evan Bracken

MAKING A FLOORCLOTH is an exciting and surprisingly easy process that offers a unique opportunity to create a functional and personalized floor covering for a special place in your home. Thanks to the development of water-based painting products, creating a floorcloth is far simpler and faster than it once was. With only modest sewing and painting skills, it's realistic to expect to design your floorcloth one week and enjoy it in your home the next!

The craft of making floorcloths is centuries old, and there is no single, *correct* way to produce these rugs. Most contemporary floorcloth artists are self taught (or they learned from someone who was) and have developed methods and combinations of materials that work for them. The guidelines in this book draw on the experiences of more than 100 artists who have spent decades making and experimenting with floorcloths. For beginners and advanced practitioners alike, the methods and materials suggested here offer a relatively simple and dependable means for creating beautiful and lasting floor coverings.

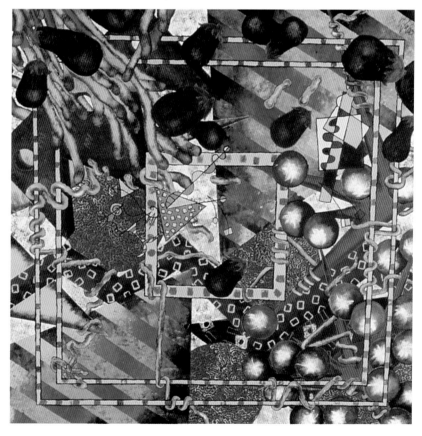

Previous page: Kathy Cooper, *Black and White Checks*, 96" x 150" (2.4 x 3.8 m), hand-painted and stenciled acrylics
Photograph: Gordon Beall

Top: Deeda Hull, *Etruscan Fish*, 6' x 6' (1.8 x 1.8 m), hand-painted acrylics
Photograph: Tom Osgood

Bottom: Marci Forbes, *Untitled*, 4' x 4' (1.2 x 1.2 m), hand-painted acrylics
Photograph: Doug Cox

## UNDERSTANDING THE MEDIUM

One of the basic ingredients of every floor-cloth is paint. Although floorcloths can be made using either water- or oil-based paint, the instructions in this book are based on using only latex, acrylic, and other water-based products. Because of the unpredict-ability of mixing materials that are chemically different, it's best not to use both water- and oil-based products on a single project. Cracking, peeling, and clouding are just some of the problems that can result.

As well as being chemically compatible, acrylics and other water-based primers, paints, and sealers simplify the painting process because of their comparatively quick drying time and ease of cleanup—requiring only soap and water, rather than oil-based solvents. Acrylic products also are user- and environ-mentally friendly, emitting fewer toxic fumes than oil-based products. If you're particularly sensitive to fumes, however, you may find that even some acrylics have an undesirable odor: ammonia is a by-product of an ingredient used to make some water-based products more liq-uid and quicker to dry. Always be sure your work space has adequate ventilation.

Used together, acrylic primers, paints, and sealers create a chemically compatible, flexi-ble, and durable surface. Your rug will have a soft, leathery texture that feels comfortable underfoot. Not only will it lie flat on a variety of floors, but it also can be easily rolled for storage or shipment.

## MATERIALS

The basic materials and tools needed to create a floorcloth are relatively commonplace and can be found in most homes or obtained at local hardware stores. Some specialized mate-rials may be needed, depending upon the sur-face design technique you choose to decorate your rug, but even these can be located today with relative ease in craft and hobby shops or at mass merchandise stores. There also are a number of mail-order sources.

### CANVAS

The type of canvas used for floorcloths is referred to commercially as a "numbered

*Top: In addition to raw can-vas, the materials needed for making a floorcloth include (approximately in rows) paste wax, acrylic paints, paint pens, salt, liquid nonskid back-ing, spray paints, acrylic sealer, acrylic paints, gloss medium, paint conditioner, matte medium, latex paints, and gesso.*

*Bottom: Susan Robertson, Cat Fantasy, 12" x 18" (30.5 x 45.5 cm), silk-screened water-based inks*

*Photograph: Mary Messick*

*Cracking, the problem most frequently cited by floorcloth makers, can result from combining paint materials that have different (and incompatible) chemical properties. To prevent cracking, use primers, paints, and sealers from the same chemical family, either water- or oil-based (water-based materials are recommended in this book). This assures that each layer will have the same degree of flexibility as its neighbors and will be less likely to dry or change at different rates, which is what leads to cracking.*

duck," and it comes in even-numbered weights from 4 (the heaviest) to 12 (the lightest). For all of the projects in this book, #10 canvas is recommended. It's fairly flexible, weighing roughly 15 ounces per yard (465 g/m), and has a medium-rough texture. It is available up to 120 inches (3 m) wide.

Some contemporary floorcloths are made of a heavier weight canvas, particularly if they're not going to be hemmed. The recommended #10 canvas, however, is easier to handle, more readily available, less expensive, and more easily sewn with a home machine than heavier

Top: Marjorie Atwood, *Red Mosaic*, 6' x 9' (1.8 x 2.7 m), acid-etched silver leaf and latex
Photograph: Scott Miller

Bottom: Charles Goforth, *Music Room*, 8' x 10' (2.4 x 3 m), hand-painted acrylics with oil glaze
Photograph: Fred Jacobs

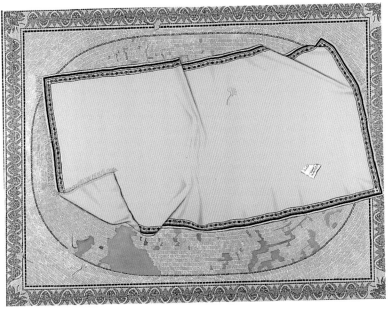

## THEN AND NOW

*The earliest floorcloths were made with oil-based products and other materials, which dictated the techniques necessary for constructing a floorcloth. For example, stretching, sizing, and sanding were required (respectively) to expose the canvas fibers, seal them from the destructive properties of oils, and to smooth out the fiber hairs and create a smooth surface.*

*Although today's improved products make many of these steps unnecessary, some contemporary floorcloth artists continue to work in oils and thus still incorporate some of the older techniques. Following is a description taken from an 1800s household advice manual for making floorcloths with oil-based products:*

"Lengths of [coarse jute or flax], 25 to 30 yards long and 8 yards wide, would be tightly stretched on a vertical frame. Both surfaces were then covered with hot size or starch to stiffen and seal the fabric. Once thoroughly dry, the entire surface was rubbed smooth with flat pieces of pumice stone. Then the first coat of paint was applied to both sides. Since the paint was too thick for application with a brush, it was applied with a trowel, much as plaster is. After drying several days, the painted surfaces were smoothed with pumice. This process was repeated four to nine times until the final coat, of thinner, higher-quality paint was applied with a brush. At this point, the floorcloth, weighing 2 to 5 pounds per square yard, resembled a flexible, well-tanned leather hide. The side of the floorcloth to be decorated was again sanded, and those cloths of premium quality were sanded and painted yet again. Patterns in oil colors were frequently applied with 8- to 24-inch square maple wood printing blocks. Numerous blocks were required for a complicated or multicolor pattern—a different block for each color or design element. Patterns were applied from selvage to selvage, printed with all the colors required for the patterns. It was possible for a skilled worker to stamp up to 150 yards per day. On narrow widths, intended for stair or hall coverings, the pattern could be machine printed. Once the entire process was completed, the surface was varnished and dried thoroughly before rolling for shipping."

*(Encyclopedia of Dry Goods, George S. Cole, The Carpet Trade, October 1875.)*

weights. It's well suited to floorcloths in all respects. A #12 canvas can be used but feels thinner; a preprimed canvas called "floorcloth canvas" can be purchased ready to use, but it's also very thin.

You can obtain #10 medium-rough weight canvas at most art supply stores or by mail order. Other possible sources include awning, tent, and marine suppliers; consult your telephone directory under these and other similar categories.

At the time your canvas is cut, ask that it be rolled onto a tube. Canvas is not forgiving of casual handling and tends to show where it has been folded or creased; these creases can be difficult to remove from canvas that is not being stretched. If you're having a large canvas shipped to you and creases are inevitable, take it to a commercial dry cleaner before you attempt to paint on your cloth and have it pressed and rolled onto a tube for you to transport home. Do not attempt to wash the canvas, as that will soften it, shrink it, and add more wrinkles. Ignore any dirt or smudges on the canvas, since these will be covered by layers of primer and paint.

Cotton canvas doesn't have a *right* and *wrong* side, but should there be a difference in the texture between the two sides of your material, select the smoother side for your painted surface.

## HEMMING

When cutting a piece of canvas for a floorcloth, you must allow some extra fabric for hemming, shrinkage (caused by the application of paint), and measurement variations. An extra 4 inches (10 cm) on both length and width should be added for small to medium rugs. For large floorcloths, add sufficient yardage to accommodate shrinkage of 3 percent.

A sewn hem is highly recommended for durability and to keep the floorcloth's edges from curling. Sewing allows you to fold under a minimal amount of canvas, creating a narrow hem that is relatively inconspicuous on the face of the rug. A sewn hem also maintains the canvas tension, lays flat on the floor, doesn't require priming on the back, and eliminates glue fumes and burned fingers from a glue gun.

Some people prefer a glued hem, using either contact cement or hot glue. To achieve a crisp edge with a glued hem, the canvas should be primed on both sides. The earliest floorcloths weren't hemmed at all; their edges were simply coated and stiffened with paint.

### SEWING LARGE CANVASES

Sewing a large piece of canvas is tricky, requiring much rolling and unrolling to move the canvas easily without creasing it. One solution for large canvases is to buy the material from an awning company and have it hemmed there. Hemming large pieces yourself requires two people and a large table, and the canvas is easier to handle and less apt to crease if you use two plastic tubes to roll and unroll the fabric as you would a scroll.

Top: Evergreene Painting Studios, detail, sisal rug, full size is 10' x 20' (3 x 6.1 m), hand-painted and stenciled acrylics
Photograph: Michael Imlay

Bottom: Susan Warlick, *Colonial Runner*, 5' x 17' (1.5 x 5.2 m), marbled oils
Photograph: Bob Skalkowski

### SEAMS

Most floorcloth makers prefer not to seam canvas in order to create large rugs. Matching two pieces of cloth can lead to a variety of technical problems. Canvas is woven up to 12 feet (3.7 m) wide and can be purchased in any length. When at all possible, work on one large piece of canvas.

### GESSO

The first step in preparing your canvas is to prime it with a coat of acrylic gesso. Priming readies the surface for paint by sealing the surface from moisture, it creates a white ground that reflects and brightens colors, and it builds an even surface on which to paint. The water in acrylic gesso shrinks the canvas slightly as it dries, producing a tight, dense backing.

Before using it, gesso must be diluted to the proper consistency. A 3.5-to-1 ratio of gesso to water works well when applying the primer with a roller. The diluted gesso should resemble slightly thinned, well-stirred sour cream.

Diluted at this rate, a quart (liter) of gesso covers approximately 50 square feet (4.9 sq. m). Store any excess in an air-tight, plastic container to prevent evaporation and rust.

Gesso should be applied generously and worked into the canvas fibers with a roller. Take care to dilute properly: primer that is too thin can buckle the unstretched canvas as well as raise the fabric texture. If this happens, wait until the primer is dry, sand it lightly with a fine-grit sandpaper, and apply another light coat of gesso. Primer that is too thick won't bond well with the canvas and may peel off later.

### FLAT EXTERIOR LATEX PAINT

Exterior latex paint, which is used for the floorcloth's background color or base coat, is formulated with a high acrylic resin content, enabling it to withstand extreme climatic changes without cracking. It offers the greatest flexibility of all available latex paints and thus is highly suitable for floorcloths.

For painting techniques that require longer working times, a low-sheen (also called *eggshell*) latex is recommended for the background color. The slight sheen adds hardness to the base coat, which causes the subsequent layer of paint to sit on the surface and not soak in and dry as quickly. By contrast, flat

Left: Marjorie Atwood, *Wild Things,* 9' x 12' (2.7 x 3.6 m), gold leaf with oils
Photograph: Scott Miller

Right: Ben Jennings, *Marbleized Tile Wall-to-Wall Floorcloth,* 9' x 16' (2.7 x 4.9 m), marbled latex and acrylics

paint absorbs paint applied on top of it, causing the second coat to dry faster.

## ARTIST'S ACRYLIC PAINTS

Artist's acrylic paints come in tubes in a wide range of colors and are available at art supply stores and from mass merchants. They are rich, concentrated colorants that are convenient to use, quick drying, and nonyellowing. Their adhesive qualities make them excellent for use with collage.

Acrylics can be used straight from the tube, and they don't change color when dry. They can be made more translucent by mixing them in small amounts with a matte medium. For fine detail work, add a touch of water to make a more liquid paint.

When dry, acrylic paints are insoluble, which means they can easily be painted over without smearing or lifting. (Unlike acrylics, other water-based paints such as watercolors, gouache, and poster paints are water soluble even when dry and will bleed if painted over.) Because they become insoluble, do not allow acrylics to dry on your brush. Wash the brush immediately after use with soap and water or leave it soaking in water until you're ready to use it again.

To choose between latex and acrylic paints, consider several factors. Latex is less expensive and often the better choice for covering large surfaces; because it's premixed and more controllable, latex provides more solid (opaque) coverage. Acrylic, because it's concentrated, offers more intense colors and more variation in tones (irregularities) within a single application, which can be desirable for decorative painting.

## PAINT PENS

Combining tool and material in one, paint pens are quick and convenient for creating details, drawing, or writing. They're available in a variety of colors, tip widths, and brands. Because brands handle differently from one another, practice using new pens on scraps of canvas to get the feel of the pen as the paint flows through its tip. You can use either acrylic or oil-based pens; the amount of paint applied is insufficient to pose any compatibility problems.

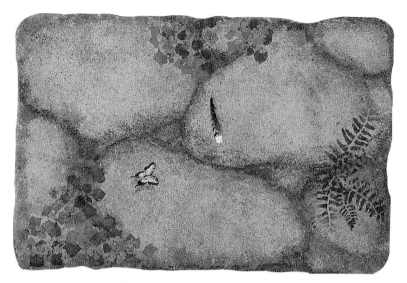

Top: Pat Scheible, *Garden Path*, 24" x 38" (61 x 96.5 cm), hand-painted acrylics on the back side of linoleum
Photograph: Evan Bracken

Bottom: Pamela Marwede, *Cat Floorcloth*, 4'x 6' (1.2 x 1.8 m), hand-painted acrylics
Photograph: Alan Ulmer

Permanent laundry markers offer an alternative to paint pens. Do *not* substitute water-based markers; varnish will cause them to bleed.

### MATTE OR GLOSS MEDIUM

Matte medium and gloss medium are acrylic polymers that are mixed with acrylic paint to make the color more translucent without thinning the paint. (Water makes paint runny; acrylic medium maintains the consistency of the paint.) You can add as much medium as you like to the paint until you get the desired degree of translucence.

### PAINT CONDITIONER

Latex paint conditioners slow the drying time of paint and prolong the existence of a wet, workable surface. They're similar to matte medium but more liquid. As a result, they add greater fluidity to paint than an acrylic medium does. Use them sparingly to thin latex paint when extra time is needed to work the surface. Conditioners increase drying time by absorbing moisture from the air. Used in too large quantities, the paint may not dry completely or may become tacky during periods of high humidity. Be sure to follow the manufacturer's instructions.

Kathy Cooper, *Hawaiian Flowers and Stripes*, 30" x 36" (76 x 91.5 cm), hand-painted acrylics
Photograph: Tom Cooper

### WATER-BASED SEALER (VARNISH)

Adding multiple coats of sealer (or varnish) on top of your painted surface is necessary to maintain its beauty and durability. Sealer pre-

vents the paint from absorbing dirt and stains, seals the design, creates a uniform level of gloss over the entire rug, and adds protective layers that can stand up to years of cleaning. Because water-based varnishes are nonyellowing, they may be used over dark- and light-colored paints without concern for changing the color of the underlying paint.

Acceptable water-based sealers include water-soluble acrylic varnish, polyurethane, and numerous other water-based polymer finishes. Select one that is compatible with the paint you're using. Sealers come in several sheens, ranging from matte to high gloss. In general, the higher the gloss or sheen, the harder the surface. To obtain most of the durability advantages of a gloss finish with somewhat less shine, choose a low-sheen finish.

### LIQUID RUBBER BACKING

Nonskid products painted onto the back of your floorcloth provide an element of safety, keeping the rug from slipping as you step on it. A rubber backing also protects the raw canvas back from dirt and moisture.

There are several nonskid rubber backing products on the market, ranging in coverage from 12 to 15 square feet per quart (1.2 to 1.5 sq. m/l). For ease of application, the backing can be rolled onto the canvas and, while still wet, washed up with water.

### PASTE WAX

A final coat of paste wax protects the finish on a rug from dirt and air—it's worth the extra time to apply it. Be sure to get clear, nonyellowing (bowling alley-type) wax. A wax with a yellow tint is acceptable for darker rugs but isn't recommended for rugs with a white background.

# BASIC TOOLS

Regardless of the design you choose for your floorcloth, the measuring and sewing tools will remain the same; however, painting and other tools can vary, depending upon the surface design technique you select. Listed below are the tools you'll need to make a simple floorcloth, such as the checkerboard design described step by step in chapter 3. To create the surface design techniques in chapter 5 or make the projects in chapter 6, you'll also need some specialized tools and materials, which are listed in those chapters with the instructions for each technique and project.

## WORK SPACE

~ Flattened, corrugated cardboard box to cover work surface

~ Drop cloth

## PAINTING TOOLS

~ Hard-lead (light) pencil or white chalk for marking patterns and hemlines on your canvas

~ Large clean paint or coffee can for mixing gesso and water

~ Mixing sticks or paddles

~ 2 clean paint roller trays, one for gesso, one for nonskid rubber backing

~ 9-inch (23 cm) roller with medium-rough cover for applying gesso

~ 9-inch (23 cm) foam roller cover for rolling on rubber backing

~ 3-inch (7.5 cm) flat synthetic bristle brush for applying latex base coat

~ 2-inch (5 cm) flat synthetic bristle brush for applying varnish

~ Plastic lids or meat trays for mixing artist's acrylic paints

~ Water bucket for washing brushes or sponges

~ Painter's masking tape (lower tack than standard masking tape, for easy removal) for masking areas you want to shield from paint

Top: Barbara Benson, detail, *Frozen in Time*, full size is 60" x 76" (1.5 x 1.9 m), silk-screened and hand-painted cold-water dyes, textile paints, and acrylics
Photograph: Jeff Slack

Bottom: To make a floorcloth, you will need these basic tools (approximately in rows): hair dryer, plastic lids and meat trays, art gum eraser, scissors, white glue, clean rags, sponges, water bucket, carpenter's framing square, painter's masking tape, 3" (7.5 cm) and 2" (5 cm) flat synthetic bristle brushes (house-painting brushes), stencil brush, pencil, T-square, flattened cardboard box, paint-mixing paddles, drop cloth, clean empty paint cans, 9" (23 cm) medium-rough roller, 9" (23 cm) foam roller, roller trays, polyester thread, heavy-duty sewing machine needles, and sewing machine.

~ Hair dryer (optional) for speed-drying acrylic paint

~ 2 sponges for cleanup and paint application (optional)

~ Paint pens, stencil brush, and comb or pastry tool (optional) for creating simple designs

## MEASURING TOOLS

~ Large metal ruler or T-square for measuring and marking border and hemline

~ Metal carpenter's framing square for corners

~ Art gum eraser

~ Sharp scissors

## SEWING TOOLS

~ Sewing machine with the ability to sew on denim

~ Heavy-duty sewing machine needle

~ Regular presser foot and hem guide

~ White thread, 100% polyester

~ White glue

~ Iron

## OTHER TOOLS

~ Soft rags for applying and buffing paste wax

Top: Hilary Law, placemats, 13" x 18" (33 x 45.5 cm), hand-painted latex and acrylics
Photograph: David Caras

Bottom: Fran Rubinstein, *Games*, 6' x 6' (1.8 x 1.8 m), hand-painted acrylics
Photograph: Bill Lemke

# PREPARING
# A WORK SPACE

Making a floorcloth doesn't require a professional work space—simply a clean area that can remain undisturbed for the duration of your project. The amount of space required by your project will vary according to the size of the floorcloth you choose to make. For a small rug about 3 by 4 feet (.9 x 1.2 m), a dining-size table or a clean basement floor will work fine.

Choose an area of your home that is relatively dust free, with good lighting (either natural or artificial) and a source of electricity to run a sewing machine, hair dryer, and iron. You also will want sufficient heat to prevent your paints from freezing. Ready access to water is desirable, although a bucket or two of clean water to wash your brushes will suffice.

Floorcloths can be made on a variety of surfaces, from the floor to the wall (by stapling the canvas directly to the wall or to a frame). A table that is thigh high works well and relieves the strain on your back. Prevent spatters on the furniture and

floors in your work space by covering them with a drop cloth or plenty of newspapers.

To protect your work surface and make the floorcloth easier to work on, pad the work surface with a flattened corrugated cardboard box. The smooth surface allows the canvas to slide around easily without rippling as you work on it from different sides. A large box from the grocery store or an appliance box works well. If you have trouble flattening the box, try cutting it apart and using a single panel or taping sections together to make a

Top: Cristina Acosta, *Fiesta Flowers*, 3' x 5' (.9 x 1.5 m), hand-painted acrylics
Photograph: Loren Irving

Left: Specialized tools for decorating a floorcloth include (approximately in rows) combing tool, cuticle scissors, ice cube tray, small cut sponges, dehydrated sponge, plastic foam sheets and packing foam, wooden block, neoprene, rope, collage items, photographs, plastic stencil film, specially cut sponge (leaf), rubber stamps, ½" (1.5 cm) flat bristle brush, #6 and #3 round brushes, Chinese hake brush, mat knife, contact cement, silk screen and squeegee, tissue paper, textured screens, cotton swabs, squeeze bottles, 1½" (4 cm) flat bristle brush, #2 bright bristle brush, ½" (1.5 cm) flat bristle brush, ½" (1.5 cm) foam brush, brayer, small sheet of glass, self-adhesive paper, picked foam roller, natural (sea) sponges, spray mister, pastry crimper, air brush, chamois, electric iron, C clamps, and electric drill.

larger panel. Your full canvas needs to be able to lie flat on the work surface with enough extra space around the canvas to make it convenient to handle.

A separate small table or shelf for paints and tools is also helpful if you're working above the floor.

Adequate ventilation is important, even for a home project made with acrylic paints. Choose a space that can be well ventilated; it's a good idea to keep a fan running to circulate the air, but don't let it blow directly on your work. For any technique that might create airborne particles or fumes, such as airbrushing or spray painting, move your work space into the open air and use a respirator.

With these few preparations in place, you're ready to begin making your own floorcloths.

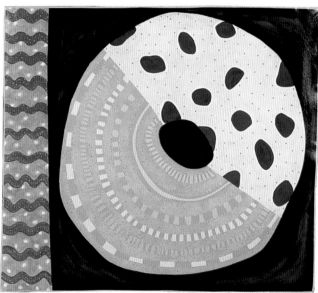

Top: Shari Cornish, *Lulu's Day Off*, 39" x 42" (99 x 106.5 cm), silk-screened fabric pigment on industrial felt
Photograph: B. Miller

Bottom: Hilary Law, *Untitled*, 60" x 62" (1.5 x 1.6 m), hand-painted acrylics and latex
Photograph: David Caras

Right: Heather Allen, *23 Broomfield*, 47" x 72" (1.2 x 1.8 m), hand-painted and silk-screened acrylics, textile inks, and colored pencils
Photograph: John Lucas

# CHAPTER 3

# MAKING A FLOORCLOTH
# STEP BY STEP

THE FOLLOWING INSTRUCTIONS will walk you through the process of making a 30- by 42-inch (76 x 106.5 cm) floorcloth with a simple checkerboard design. The resulting rug is suitable for a kitchen, bath, or entry-way—large enough to make a design statement in your home, yet small enough to be made in a modest work space.

The checkerboard design itself is as classic as they come, yet ever so contemporary. The pattern was a standard design in the heyday of floorcloths—the 1700s and 1800s—when it was intended to mimic the classic elegance of a marble floor. An historic approach might be to paint the rug in black and white or black and hunter green. For a more contemporary feel, try one of the designs shown in the examples on pages 42 and 43 or make up your own color combination. Your personal style can be expressed further by your choice of border color and decoration. You can keep it simple with a band of another color, add a bit of whimsy with a combed edge, repeat the checked theme with rows of smaller-scale checks, or pick up a color or design theme from the room in which you plan to use the rug—just to name a few of your options. The possibilities are endless.

Previous page: Constance Miller, *Forest Floor*, 3' x 3' (91.5 x 91.5 cm), sponged and stenciled acrylics
Photograph: Michael Seidl

Right: Tara Loughlin, *Pomegranate*, 72" x 102" (1.8 x 2.6 m), stippled and hand-painted oils
Photograph: Kevin Brusie

## STEP 1: PRIMING—
## PREPARING THE CANVAS TO PAINT

**For this step you will need:** canvas, scissors, tape measure or ruler, iron, 1 quart (.9 l) acrylic gesso, 1 gallon (3.8 l) mixing container, water, paint mixing paddle, paint roller with a medium-nap cover, paint roller tray.

Begin by cutting or purchasing a piece of canvas the size of the desired finished rug plus at least 4 inches (10 cm) on length and width to accommodate the hem and shrinkage. For this rug, begin with a piece of canvas approximately 34 x 46 inches (86.5 x 117 cm).

Lay the canvas on a clean, padded work surface and lightly iron it, using the steam and cotton settings. Take care to eliminate all creases.

Dilute the acrylic gesso with water at a 3.5 to 1 ratio (i.e., 3½ cupfuls of gesso to 1 cupful of water) for the proper working consistency. At this rate, the entire quart (liter) of gesso will cover approximately 50 square feet (4.9 sq. m). You won't need that much to prime this sample rug, but pour a generous amount into the tray, as some of it will be absorbed by the roller. Save the excess for a later project.

In a large, clean coffee can or paint bucket, mix the gesso and water with a paint paddle until the water has been completely absorbed. The resulting primer should be the consistency of thinned sour cream—thin enough to roll with a paint roller, but not watery. At this consistency, the gesso creates a smooth, paintable surface (any unevenness will be eliminated by subsequent layers). Primer that is too thin raises the grain of the fabric, creating a rough surface. If this happens, let the primer and canvas dry thoroughly, sand lightly with a fine-grit sandpaper, and apply another light coat of gesso.

Using a roller with a medium-rough nap, roll the gesso onto the canvas, working back and forth across the center of the fabric first and then rolling from the center to the edges (figure 1). For applying gesso to large surfaces, a roller works faster than a brush, and it presses the primer into the fibers, providing more thorough coverage. As you roll the gesso onto the canvas, take care not to ripple

the loose fabric. Allow the gesso to soak into the canvas; then smooth out any high spots and eliminate any ridges with the roller. Allow the canvas to dry overnight or until the primer is completely dry.

*Tip: To save time and work on your next project, a gesso-covered roller can be stored in a plastic bag in the freezer and thawed before you need it.*

Callahan McDonough, *Chair Series*, 52" x 60" (1.3 x 1.5 m), hand-painted acrylics
Photograph: Evan Bracken

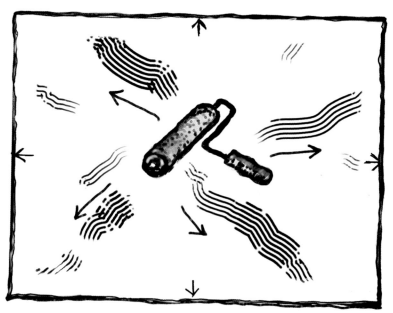

Figure 1

## STEP 2: APPLYING THE BACKGROUND COLOR (BASE COAT)

**For this step you will need:** flat exterior latex house paint in the desired background color, 3-inch (7.5 cm) synthetic bristle brush. *Note: if you plan to use decorating techniques that require time to work the paint, such as glazing or combing, select a low-sheen rather than a flat latex.*

Brush a coat of the latex paint over the entire primed canvas, being careful to work out drips and puddles to leave a smooth, flat surface. As with the primer, brush from the center outward, carrying your paint over the entire canvas but taking care to keep the paint from seeping under the edges (to keep your work surface and the back of the rug clean). Allow the paint to dry overnight or until it feels dry to the touch. This can take as little as an hour or two on a warm, dry day. Don't worry if your base coat seems a bit uneven — you'll add a second background coat later.

## STEP 3: MARKING THE HEM FOLD LINE

**For this step you will need:** your primed and painted canvas, hard-lead pencil, large metal T-square or ruler, carpenter's framing square, scissors.

Select the longest side of the canvas that appears to be straight (side A) and, using your ruler, pencil a 42-inch (106.5 cm) line about 1 inch (2.5 cm) in from the edge of the canvas. Make a small dot at each end of the line. Be sure to leave at least an inch (2.5 cm) of canvas beyond each dot for the hem.

Next lay the framing square along the penciled line, with the square's left perpendicular edge on the left dot (figure 2). Lay the ruler on top of the framing square's perpendicular arm, creating a continuous straight edge running the length of side B and at a right angle to side A. Pencil a 30-inch (76 cm) line along the straight edge, and make a dot at each end of the line.

Repeat this process, using the dot on the right end of the line on side A, to create a second 30-inch (76 cm) line along side D. Make a dot at the end of this line.

Complete the rectangle by connecting the dots at the ends of the lines on sides B and D to create the line on side C.

Before going on, check all your measurements. You should have two lines exactly 42 inches (106.5 cm) long on sides A and C and two 30-inch (76 cm) lines on sides B and D; if you don't, back up, remeasure, and recheck each corner with the framing square.

Using a dotted line, draw a second rectangle 5/8 inches (1.6 cm) outside the first. Cut along the dotted line with scissors, leaving only the 30- by 42-inch (76 x 106.5 cm) rug with a 5/8-inch (1.6 cm) hem allowance all around (figure 3).

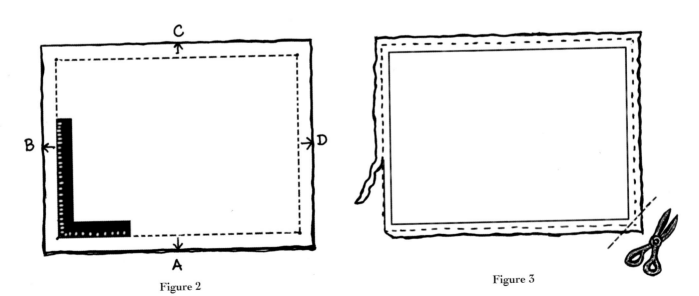

Figure 2

Figure 3

Trim the point off each corner, cutting halfway between the outside point and the corner of your rectangle.

## STEP 4: SEWING THE HEM

**For this step you will need:** sewing machine, regular presser foot, hem guide, brand new heavy-duty needle suitable for denim, white 100% polyester thread, white glue.

With your machine set for the longest stitch and the tension set for heavy denim, practice sewing on a scrap of canvas folded to double thickness. Adjust the tension as necessary to produce smooth, even stitches. If you use a brand new needle, most sturdy new and old machines can sew through a double layer of canvas, since it is very similar to sewing on denim. However, if your machine is straining (or if you don't have a sewing machine), you can have an upholsterer hem the canvas for you inexpensively.

Adjust your hem guide for a ¼-inch (5 mm) hem. If you don't have a hem guide, fabricate a visual guide by extending the ¼ -inch (5 mm) mark on the needle plate with a piece of masking tape.

To make sewing easier, begin at any edge and gently roll the canvas into a loose tube, painted side out. With the painted side down, fold the hem toward the roll (unpainted side to unpainted side) along your pencilled hem line (figure 4).

Position the rolled canvas to the left of the presser foot. Beginning at the corner farthest from you, lock the presser foot into position just in from the edge of the corner, backstitch to secure the thread, and sew slowly along the folded hem, ¼ inch (5 mm) in from the edge. Keep your line of stitching as straight as possible and fold the hem to the left along the pencilled hem line as you go. When you reach the next corner, backstitch a few stitches, and sew forward, completely off the canvas. Clip the threads.

Continue to reroll the canvas and repeat the hemming process on adjacent sides until all four edges are hemmed and you are back at your starting point. Trim all the loose threads.

Finish the hem by running a thin bead of white glue just under the lip of the hem to seal it securely and prevent the rubber backing (to be applied later) from seeping under the hem edge and creating a thick spot. Allow the glue to dry; then lightly press the hem and back of the floorcloth with a warm iron.

## STEP 5: APPLYING A SECOND COAT OF BACKGROUND COLOR

**For this step you will need:** flat exterior latex paint from step 2 and 3-inch (7.5 cm) synthetic bristle brush.

Lay your hemmed floorcloth hem side down on your work surface and paint on a second coat of the background color. Take care once again to brush from the center outward to keep the paint from seeping under the edges. Allow this coat to dry.

Deeda Hull, *Etruscan Ram's Head*, 2' x 3' (61 x 91.5 cm), hand-painted acrylics
Photograph: Tom Osgood

**Figure 4**

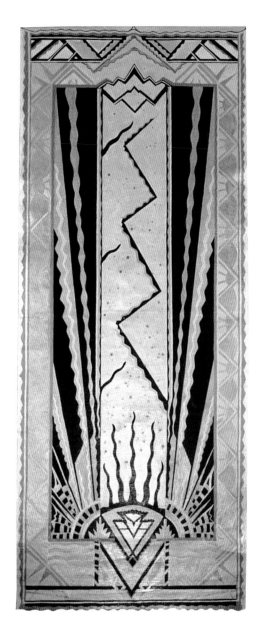

Top left: Brigid Finucane, *Deco Doors*, 34" x 83" (.8 x 2.1 m), stenciled and hand-painted acrylic and metallic paints

Top right: Pat Burgee, *Untitled*, 48" x 70" (1.2 x 1.8 m), marbled latex
Photograph: Michael Houstle

Bottom: Sue Hardy, *Cheeta Floorcloth*, 4' x 6' (1.2 x 1.8 m), hand-painted and stenciled acrylics

## STEP 6: DRAWING THE DESIGN

**For this step you will need:** hard-lead pencil, art gum eraser, T-square or metal ruler.

First measure and mark the center point of each edge of the rug; then draw a line connecting the two center points opposite each other on the shorter edges and another line connecting the two center points opposite each other on the longer edges. Where these lines intersect is the center point of the rug itself.

Beginning at the rug's center point, mark at 6-inch (15 cm) intervals along both of the lines just drawn. Mark corresponding 6-inch (15 cm) intervals on all sides of the rug, beginning at the center point of each edge (figure 5).

Now use your long ruler and pencil to draw a line connecting each row of horizontal and vertical marks. Your lines should form a grid of 24 6-inch (15 cm) squares, four one way and six the other, with a 3-inch (7.5 cm) border all around.

## STEP 7: PAINTING THE DESIGN

**For this step you will need:** painter's blue masking tape, flat latex paint from step 2, sponge, design color paints, desired painting tool (clean sponge, stencil brush, or other stiff bristle brush), matte medium, touch-up tools.

To protect the border and define the squares, apply painter's tape around the outside edge of the entire checkerboard grid. Then run

tape around the outside of every other square in rows 1 and 3, masking off a checkerboard of perfect squares to paint (figure 6).

Press the tape down tightly to prevent the paint from seeping under it; then seal the edge by lightly sponging along the tape lines with the background color. The masking tape has, in effect, formed a stencil. Allow the paint to dry. *Tip: To speed up drying time, use a hand-held hair dryer.*

Select a color for the alternate squares in your checkerboard and pour a small amount of this paint into a jar lid or other small container. If desired, you can make the paint more translu-

Barbara Benson, *Spring Blueberry Barrens*, 38" x 53" (1 x 1.3 m), silk-screened and hand-painted textile paints, mineral dyes, and acrylics
Photograph: Thuss Photography

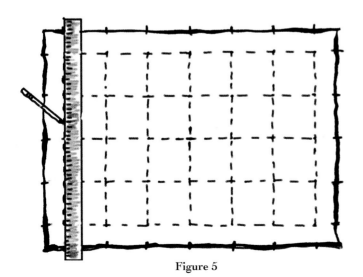

**Figure 5**

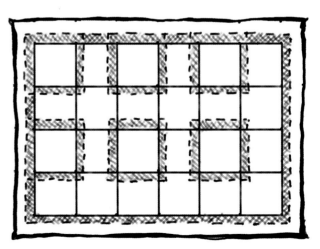

**Figure 6**

cent by adding some matte medium. (Do not use water as a thinning agent; water will make the paint runny.)

Before painting on your rug, practice stenciling on a scrap of fabric or heavy paper until you get the desired painting effect. Lightly dab the brush or sponge in the paint, and brush any excess paint onto a scrap of canvas or other neutral absorbent surface such as a brown paper bag or cardboard. This "dry brush" stenciling technique is less likely to allow the paint to seep under the tape and blur your lines.

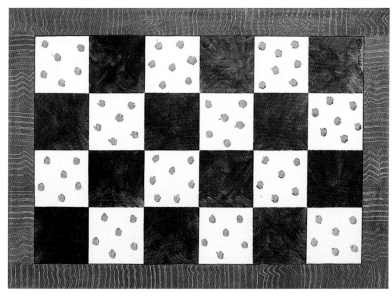

Now stencil the design color on each masked square, working the paint from the outside taped edge to the center of each square. Allow the squares to dry thoroughly.

Remove the tape around the painted squares (leaving the border tape in place), and repeat the process on rows 2 and 4, masking off the appropriate squares to create a checkerboard effect. Allow the paint to dry thoroughly; then remove all remaining tape.

To decorate the border, place painter's tape along the edge of the border on top of the recently painted squares, outlining the border for painting. Press the tape down securely, but don't seal the edges with the background color, as some of the checks are now a different color.

Paint the border in the desired color using the same dry brush technique or try another method. A few options are shown at left and opposite: a hand-painted ribbon within the border, a two-toned border with a combed pattern, a pattern of smaller checks, and a gold glaze over a contrasting color. For more ideas, refer to the surface design techniques described in chapter 5 and look at the many other floorcloths in this book.

Whatever design you choose, allow the paint to dry thoroughly; then remove the tape and, as necessary, touch up any areas by hand with the appropriate colors. At this point you can also sharpen the edges of the squares where they meet the border by using a metal ruler and a paint pen in a complementary color. Be sure to test the paint pen on a scrap before using it on your floorcloth; even a fresh pen can sometimes deposit globs of paint on the canvas. Allow all your touch-ups to dry. *Tip: If any paint has bled onto the background color, lightly scrape it off with a razor blade before touching up with background paint.*

## STEP 8: APPLYING A PROTECTIVE SEALER

**For this step you will need:** clean sponge, 2-inch (5 cm) synthetic bristle brush, satin or gloss acrylic sealer.

Using a clean damp sponge, lightly wipe the entire painted surface clean of any dust or debris. Apply the sealer according to the manufacturer's recommendations, using a synthetic bristle brush saved exclusively for this purpose. Proceed from one side of the rug to the other in long, smooth, side-by-side strokes, brushing out or blotting up puddles with paper towels as necessary. Don't be alarmed if the sealer looks milky when it's wet; it will dry clear. *Warning: Rebrushing already-painted areas increases the sheen where you brush and may result in an uneven finish; excessive brushing also can trap air, creating bubbles that will dry cloudy.*

Allow the sealer to dry according to the manufacturer's recommendations. Drying time will vary according to the type of varnish and humidity.

Repeat the sealing process from three to five times, until the painted surface feels smooth to the touch. Allow each coat to dry thoroughly before applying the next and allow the rug to cure overnight before going on to the next step.

## STEP 9: APPLYING A FINAL COAT OF PASTE WAX

**For this step you will need:** clear, non-yellowing (bowling alley) paste wax, several soft cloths.

Using a soft cloth, wipe a thin coat of paste wax over the entire sealed surface of your floorcloth. When the wax is dry, hand buff it with a clean, soft cloth until it reaches an attractive sheen.

## STEP 10: APPLYING A NONSKID RUBBER BACKING

**For this step you will need:** 1 quart (1 l) liquid rubber backing, paint roller with a foam cover, clean paint roller tray.

Pour the nonskid backing into the roller tray and evenly coat the roller. Working on the back of your floorcloth and rolling parallel to (but inside of) each hemmed edge, apply the backing around the perimeter of the raw canvas, turning the rug as you go. Then continue rolling the backing into the center of the cloth, making the coating as smooth and even as possible. Avoid getting the backing on the hem, since the rubber will not adhere well to the paint. While the backing is still wet, use a

damp cloth to remove any that has seeped onto or under the edge of the hem. Allow the backing to dry according to the manufacturer's recommendations.

Congratulations! You have just completed your floorcloth and are ready to enjoy years of use from it. You will find it a pleasure to live with and extremely durable.

*Tip: Make a note of the types of primer, paint, and sealer used on your floorcloth; knowledge of these products may be helpful when you want to make another rug or need to touch up this one with compatible materials.*

Top: Kathy Cooper, *Checkerboard with Rooster,* 30" x 42" (76 x 106.5 cm), stenciled, glazed, and hand-painted acrylics with photo transfer
Photograph: Evan Bracken

Bottom: Kathy Cooper, *Checkerboard with Gold Glaze and Leaves,* 30" x 42" (76 x 106.5 cm), stenciled, glazed, and block-printed acrylics
Photograph: Evan Bracken

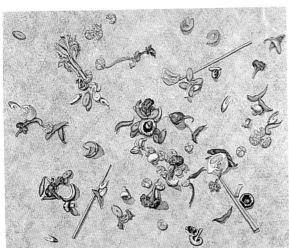

Top: Ellie Ernst, *Pastorale* (adaptation of antique scagliola table top), 54" x 180" (1.4 x 4.6 m), hand-painted acrylics
Photograph: Ransy Morr

Center left: Ginny Speirs, *Stir Fry*, 30" x 36" (76 x 91.5 cm), ragged and hand-painted oils
Photograph: Evan Bracken

Center right: Joan Weissman, *Untitled*, 42" x 60" (1.1 x 1.5 m), hand-painted latex
Photograph: Damian Andrus

Bottom: Alan Vaughn, *Triangle Chase*, 33" x 77" (.8 x 2 m), hand-painted acrylics

# CHAPTER 4

# DESIGN CONSIDERATIONS

You've decided that a floorcloth is just the accent your home needs; but what will it look like? Don't worry if you can't come up with an idea off the top of your head—even design professionals don't work that way. This chapter will walk you through the decisions you'll need to make concerning location, use, size, design motifs, colors, and style preferences, and then help you translate your design onto canvas.

You'll need only a few tools: photographs of the room where the floorcloth will be, a file to hold ideas, and paper and pencil to help you think visually. At the end of the chapter you'll find a design checklist to help you work through your options.

## Location, Location, Location

The first—but not always the most obvious—step is deciding where your floorcloth will go. Your dining room may have been without a rug since you moved into your home years ago, but such a large project may be a bit too ambitious for a first effort. Think "manageable." Floorcloths are effective in the kitchen, bath, hallway, foyer, solarium, and porch. In fact, a floorcloth can go anywhere, large room or small.

The size of the work space you can devote to making your floorcloth is also a consideration. Decide where you will work to see what size rug you can accommodate.

## Sizing Up the Overall Picture

Having settled on the intended location of your new floorcloth, photograph the room from several different angles. Your photos will provide a fresh perspective that you don't get from living with the space on a daily basis.

How much of this space should your floorcloth cover? Think of the visual impact and the practical considerations. Let the rug define a space, be it a conversation area or sink splash zone. For example, for a rug that will protect the floor in front of the kitchen sink, should it be a mat size or a runner?

What design themes already exist in the room—in the wallpaper or fabrics? What colors or textures? Does the rug need to be able to hide soil? Will furniture be moved around on it?

Previous page: Kathy Cooper, *Zigzag Border with Confetti Center*, 8' x 12' (2.4 x 3.6 m), hand-painted acrylics
Photograph: Tim Fields

Kathy Cooper, *Hummingbirds and Lattice*, 3' x 12' (.9 x 3.6 m), stenciled and hand-painted acrylics
Photograph: Tim Fields

Consider traffic patterns. A floorcloth is meant to be walked on, but don't place an edge in the middle of a pathway where it might trip someone. Standard area rug sizes have evolved because they suit many purposes, but don't be afraid to customize your rug size to suit your particular needs. In fact, that's one of the benefits of making your own floorcloth—you can make it just the size and shape you want for that long, narrow bath or octagonal breakfast nook.

## CREATING A PATTERN

Once you've decided on the physical parameters of your floorcloth, make a paper pattern.

Tape newspapers together to approximate the size of the rug; then tape the pattern to the floor and look at it in relationship to the space. Take note of any doors that open on to it, furniture on or around it, traffic that will cross it, and how it fits spatially. The paper pattern will help assure that your rug is proportional to the space, useful, and safe. When you have it just right, jot down your measurements.

You can take this idea one step further by using white drawing paper for the pattern and sketching your design ideas full scale to see how they look.

Carmon Slater, *Untitled*,
12' x 12' (3.6 x 3.6 m),
hand-painted pigments
Photograph: Pete Krumhardt

## ON AND OFF THE FLOOR

### OTHER USES

*In addition to floorcloths, painted canvas translates beautifully into such unique and practical "linens" as place mats, table runners, and dresser scarves. To make a mat or runner, follow the same steps outlined for a rug, but cut the canvas to fit the new application, making sure to allow extra length and width to accommodate shrinkage and hemming.*

*Painted canvas also can be sewn into pillows, chair covers, slings for director's chairs, headboards, lamp shades, or upholstery. When sealed or protected with a commercial spray stain inhibitor, canvas is versatile and wipes clean with a damp sponge.*

### OTHER TREATMENTS

*Traditional floorcloths attain their beauty from painted designs. However, canvas also can be painted, cut into strips and woven, stitched and appliquéd to add visual and textural interest.*

Top: Rhonda Kaplan, *Double Border Tulip*, 5' x 7' (1.5 x 2.1 m), hand-painted latex
Photograph: Shelley Noble

Bottom left: Fran Rubinstein, *Tazmania*, director's chair, 36" H x 25"W x 18"D (91.5 x 63.5 x 45.5 cm), hand-painted acrylics
Photograph: Bill Lemke

Bottom right: Shari Cornish, *Xs and Os*, 34" x 38" (86.5 x 96.5 cm), silk-screened fabric pigment on industrial felt
Photograph: B. Miller

## OTHER SURFACES

*Canvas is not the only material to surrender to the artist's hand for use as a floor covering—either now or in earlier days. Several varieties of sisal (natural, woolfaced, and synthetic), as well as jute, cotton, linen, industrial felt, baize (coarsely woven wool or cotton), and linoleum have all been decorated for use underfoot.*

*Sisal can be purchased in any size and painted using many of the same techniques described here for floorcloths. Stenciling, air brushing, and spray painting are particularly effective for applying color to the rough texture of the sisal fibers.*

*The felt-backed surface of commercial-grade sheet vinyl (linoleum) is used by some artists today as a base for painted designs. It offers a handy flat surface that doesn't require the construction steps associated with canvas rugs; in addition, vinyl doesn't shrink and can be cut with pruning shears into freeform shapes. Working on the felted side, prime, paint, and seal the material as if it were canvas. Be sure to select a linoleum with minimal embossing; with time, such textures will telegraph through the rug and appear on the painted side.*

*Modern technology has given rise to numerous materials that might be appropriate surfaces for the adventurous painter. Look for nonwoven polyester feltlike fabrics, heavyweight versions of fabrics used for clothing interfacing, and rubberized or coated fabrics used for home furnishings. In fact, anything that has some heft to it, lies flat, and accepts paint offers possibilities as a floorcloth material.*

Top: Joan Weissman, table cover, 3' x 4' (.9 x 1.2 m), hand-painted latex
Photograph: Meridel Rubenstein

Center: Angie Nelson, *Ivy Wreath*, place mat, 14" x 14" (35.5 x 35.5 cm); *Quilt Block*, coaster, 4¾" x 4¾" (12 x 12 cm); hand-painted latex and acrylics
Photograph: Tatum, Toomey & Whicker

Bottom left: Joyce Barker-Schwartz, detail, *Fire Flower II*, full size is 6' x 7' (1.8 x 2.1 m), hand-painted acrylics and woven canvas
Photograph: Karen Mauch

Bottom right: Angie Nelson, *Herb Wreath*, table runner and place mat, 10" x 36" (25.5 x 91.5 cm) and 14" x 14" (35.5 x 35.5 cm); *Quilt Block*, coasters, 4-¾" x 4¾" (12 x 12 cm); hand-painted latex and acrylics
Photograph: Tatum, Toomey & Whicker

## ACCENT VS. ACCESSORY

Both the size of your rug and the design you create for it will determine whether it serves as the focal point of your room or as an accessory to an existing theme or features. For an accent, use a bold approach, such as bright and/or contrasting colors or large-scale motifs. An accent rug will be the first thing that's noticed when a person enters the room. For an accessory, take a subtle approach—softer or less contrasting colors or smaller, calmer motifs. This allows the floorcloth to blend into the room. A visitor might only realize it's a floorcloth rather than a carpet by walking on it.

To decide on the impact you want the floorcloth to create, go back to your room photos and ask yourself what your room needs. Seek a balance between serenity and movement among all the things going on in the room. Does your room need a pick-me-up? Something to tie together or unify other elements in the room? A background to show off interesting furniture or accessories? A conversation piece? Visualize the rug as each of these and decide what feels best. There is no one correct answer.

Opposite: Kathy Cooper, *Diagonal Checks with Striped Border*, 7' x 9' (2.1 x 2.7 m), hand-painted acrylics
Photograph: Tim Fields

Top: Pamela Marwede, *Untitled*, 6' x 12' (1.8 x 3.6 m), hand-painted acrylics
Photograph: Alan Ulmer

Bottom: Joyce Barker-Schwatrz, *Elements II*, 8' x 10' (2.4 x 3 m), hand-painted acrylics and woven canvas with dyed cording
Photograph: Barry Halken

## DEVELOPING DESIGN MOTIFS

Once you've determined the size and purpose of your rug and the overall feel (accent or accessory), consider the style or motifs you will use to achieve the look you want.

Design inspiration can come from anywhere. You may find it in some element of the room itself: fabrics, wallpaper, architectural features, furniture designs, accessories, or even the view out the window.

Top: Maleesa Davis, *Beaches*, 3' x 5'(.9 x 1.5 m), stippled and hand-painted acrylics

Center: Laura Rogers, *Serpentine Marble*, 3' x 5' (.9 x 1.5 m), stenciled and glazed oils
Photograph: Chandler McKaig

Bottom: Maleesa Davis, *Save My Skin*, 7' x 12' (2.1 x 3.6 m), hand-painted acrylics
Photograph: Caroll Conway

Other ideas lie in wait in books or magazines on home decor. Study these not only for current style trends, but for features and color combinations that catch your eye. Find a room you like and study it to see what elements were used to create that feeling. Are there bright, muted, or monochromatic colors? Clean lines

or curvy ones? A unified, period approach or an eclectic look? Lace and velvet or Shaker simplicity? What kind of floorcloth would contribute to the feel you're after? Clip pages and create a file for inspiration.

History can contribute a wealth of ideas too. Architectural details, old fabrics, antique floorcloth patterns, old portraits showing early floor coverings, and art history books all could lead you to age-old designs. There's no need to get stuck in history, though; you can take an old idea and

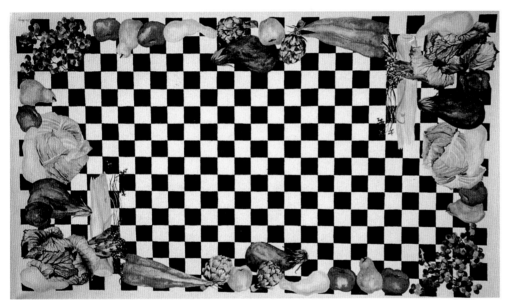

Top: Deeda Hull, *Clown Fish*, 30" x 48" (76 x 122 cm), hand-painted acrylics
Photograph: Tom Osgood

Center: Sue Hardy, *Veggie Floorcloth*, 4' x 6' (1.2 x 1.8 m), handpainted acrylics

Bottom left: Maryellen Murphy, *Farmer's Market*, 48" x 76" (1.2 x 1.9 m), ragged, sponged, and collaged acrylics with 1940s decals
Photograph: Kate Cameron

Bottom right: Fran Rubinstein, *Three Rings*, 4' x 4' (1.2 x 1.2 m), hand-painted acrylics
Photograph: Bill Lemke

Right: Laura Rogers, *Fireworks*, 3' x 5' (.9 x 1.5 m), stenciled acrylics
Photograph: Chandler McKaig

Bottom: Rhonda Kaplan, *Untitled*, 8' x 10' (2.4 x 3 m), hand-painted latex
Photograph: Jay Friedlander

color it with hues from today's palette or add a whimsical border.

Where you locate your rug will affect the placement and style of your design. For instance, if a floorcloth is to go under a glass dining table, the center will be of more interest than it would be on a rug used under a wooden table. For the glass table, your design emphasis might be on a central motif; for the wooden table, develop an eye-catching border.

## DESIGNING & SIZING BORDERS

Some rugs have borders, others do not—it's a matter of personal preference. A rug without a border is said to have an overall design. A border has several purposes: it can frame a center field; it can be the focal point of the rug itself, set off by a simpler or quieter center; it can add emphasis to a rug, often making it more noticeable; and a border can pep up a rug or calm it down.

The size of the border should be in proportion to the total piece. For example, on a small 30-by 36-inch (76 x 91.5 cm) rug, the border may be only 3 inches (7.5 cm) wide, but the border may run 12 to 18 inches (30.5 to 45.5 cm) wide on a room-size rug. Border size depends on the size of the piece and the effect you want to create.

Your border design can draw on a motif used in the body of the rug, but perhaps on a different scale; it can offer a colorful contrast to the center design; or it can pick up on another design element in the room or in an adjacent area. For example, if the kitchen has a black-and-white tile floor, a floorcloth for an

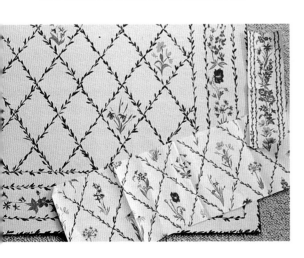

Top: Sue Bleyaert, *Trillium*, 2' x 3' (61 x 91.5 cm), hand-painted latex

Bottom left: Sue Bleyaert, *Mrs. Hooker*, 30" x 36" (76 x 91.5 cm), hand-painted latex

Bottom right: Mary Moross, *Circus*, 3' x 6' (.9 x 1.8 m), hand-painted acrylics and latex
Photograph: Ileona Saurez

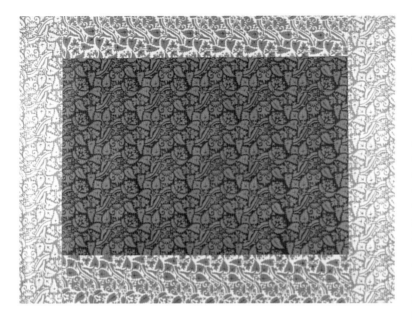

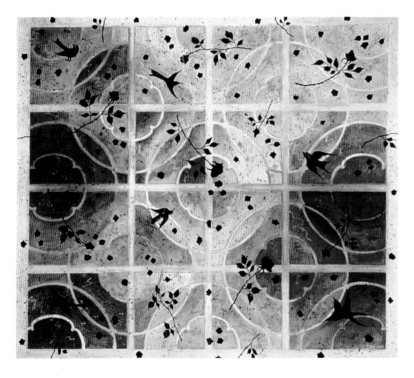

adjacent space might repeat the black-and-white theme but on a different scale—perhaps with a row of small checks or diamonds on the border. This subtle repetition suggests a relationship between the two rooms without simply copying the design.

Sketch or imagine your rug with and without a border, with borders of different widths, and with borders of similar and contrasting colors. You can use a border to try out a new decorating technique—such as sponging or combing—or to add a bit of whimsy. The sky and your imagination are your only limitations.

## COLOR BASICS

The choice of colors for your design ideas may arise from a sudden inspiration, evolve from trial and error, or seem an overwhelming impossibility. Don't despair—help is on the way.

Start your color search by looking at the photographs you took of your room. You'll quickly pick up on colors that have been used to coordinate the fabrics, wallpaper, and paints. Is there too much of a particular color? Not enough? Are there colors to avoid? Is there a color that needs more definition or one that would add an element of surprise? Consider all the colors in the room, not just the ones that first jump out. You may find that a wonderful accent color from the fabric on an arm chair or the jacket of a book on the shelf would be perfect for your floorcloth.

Color mixing is an art in itself—second nature to some and intimidating to others. In reality, it's not nearly as complicated as it may seem at first. If you think back to your early school days, the principles will be familiar. The color wheel exists as a way of understanding where colors fall in relationship to each other (adjacent or opposite) and of how we see one color when it's used with others. Following are the four basic color schemes and a few color basics to help get you started.

**Monochromatic:** This color scheme uses one color, varying it in degrees of lighter or darker shades for accent.

Top: Roger Mudre, *Blue Textile*, 3' x 4' (.9 x 1.2 m), stenciled acrylics
Photograph: Ty Hyon

Bottom: Patricia Dreher, *Blackbirds & Roses*, 8' x 9' (2.4 x 2.7 m), hand-painted and glazed acrylics
Photograph: Valerie Massey

Opposite top: Sue Bleyaert, *Dancing Fish*, 30" x 36" (76 x 91.5 cm), hand-painted latex

Opposite bottom: Joyce Barker-Schwartz, *Slightly Off Center*, 8' x 8' (2.4 x 2.4 m), hand-painted acrylics and woven canvas
Photograph: Barry Halkin

**Adjacent or Related:** This combines three colors that are adjacent to each other on the color wheel; their common color holds them together. Examples are purple, violet, and red, or yellow, yellow-orange, and orange. Adjacent color schemes create subtle variations and interest and are probably the most foolproof to use.

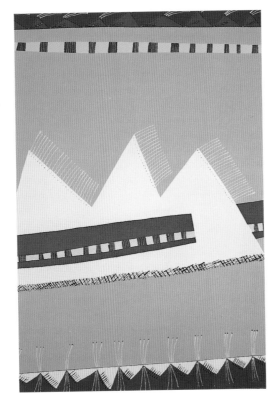

Top: Joan Weissman, *Untitled*, 42" x 60" (1 x 1.5 m), hand-painted latex
Photograph: Robert Reck

Center: Kathy Cooper, *Pink Spirals with Triangles*, 30" x 36" (76 x 91.5 cm), hand-painted acrylics
Photograph: Tom Cooper

Bottom: Kathy Cooper, *Abstract Flowers with Triangle Border*, 5' x 6' (1.5 x 1.8 m), hand-painted acrylics
Photograph: Tom Cooper

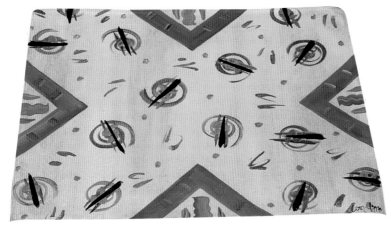

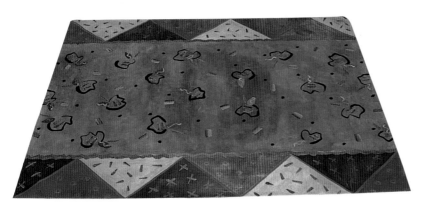

**Complementary:** This scheme pairs two colors that are directly opposite each other on the color wheel, such as blue and orange, purple and yellow, or red and green. One color should dominate. This combination will seem alive with movement and add visual drama to the space.

**Split-complementary:** This is the most complex scheme, pairing one color on the wheel with the two colors adjacent to its opposite color. Rather than balance equally, one color should dominate; 60-20-20 is a comfortable proportion. As an example, imagine hunter green as the dominant color, with accents of red and violet.

A basic color wheel or a set of Pantone color chips is a good tool to keep with your art supplies. It will help guide you to your options when you are combining or mixing colors.

When mixing paint, adding white to any color lightens the tint or shade of the color; adding black darkens the tone. Adding a touch of a complementary color can quickly subdue a color (combining equal amounts produces gray).

Yellow provides the least coverage of all colors.

On a psychological level, colors make us feel movement: yellow and red suggest action (fast-food restaurants); blue implies stability (banks, hotels); green suggests nature (environmentally-sensitive products). They also can make us feel temperature: the blue family feels cool; yellow and red families feel warm.

## SELECTING A BACKGROUND COLOR

Think of your floorcloth's background color as the backdrop to your intended design. This layer on top of your gesso primer can either serve as part of the design or ultimately be covered by other colors. Covering it is far from being a wasted effort, however; the base coat helps smooth the rough surface of the canvas, and a white base coat makes colors washed over it appear brighter and more energetic.

The type of use the rug and the room receive also can influence the background color you choose. If the room is rarely used, you need not be as concerned about dirt showing, and either light or dark colors will work.

However, for a rug that is to be in the center of a kitchen full of active children, soil-showing properties are a consideration. Be forewarned, light as well as dark colors can be a problem: light colors show dirt; dark colors show dust. A sponged background is one solution for high-traffic areas because the mottled effect helps to hide both.

When selecting colors, consider the overall effect the rug will create. Do you need to lighten a dark room? Choose a lighter overall color. Are you looking for sophistication? Then try earthy or darker hues.

Acrylic varnishes and latex paints don't all react the same way to each other. It's always a good idea, when selecting your paint and varnish, to do a small test for compatibility. If you seem to be having problems, try another brand of either the paint or the varnish. Then keep track of your results for future projects.

## SELECTING DESIGN COLORS

To arrive at the design colors in your floor-cloth, try out some combinations using colored pencils or magic markers. For inspiration, turn to your fabrics, wallpaper, and magazine clippings. Include elements of surprise with bits of color that add detail and catch the viewer's attention. Think "impact" and experiment with a palette of complementary colors; think "subtlety" and substitute adjacent colors. Try one approach for the center and another with the border. Eventually, something will strike you as being just right.

## MIXING COLORS

Once you have an idea in your mind and a small map to get there, consider the paints you will need. A basic palette includes crimson red (a blue-red), naphthol red (a warm red), medium or light cadmium yellow, ultramarine blue, white, and black. You might also want some specialty colors, such as phthalo green, phthalo blue, Hooker's green, burnt sienna, and raw umber. All can be used straight out of the tube or mixed. Don't feel guilty if you want to avoid mixing colors at first; once you start painting, you'll gain confidence and may feel inspired to experiment.

A good rule when mixing colors is to start with a small amount. Once you think you've

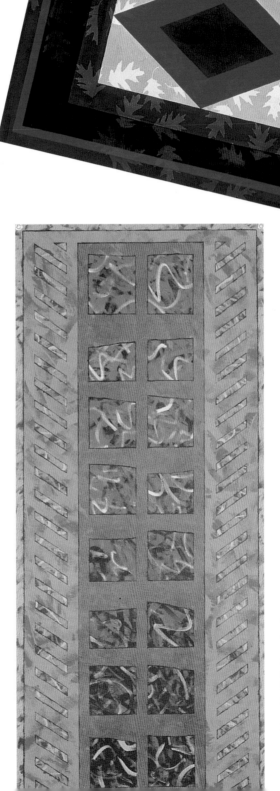

Top: Barbara Benson, *Amish Series #1*, 38" x 51" (.9 x 1.3 m), hand-painted and silk-screened textile paints and acrylics
Photograph: Thuss Photography

Bottom: Gary Mackender, *Untitled*, 36" x 78" (.9 x 2 m), masking tape with acrylics

found the right color, mix only enough for the current intended use. Acrylics dry quickly and are difficult to save for later. To achieve the same hue a second time, be sure to write down your proportions.

If all this color talk gets you feeling nervous, just think back to kindergarten and recall the exuberance you felt when smearing finger paints all over a page. When you begin to work on your floorcloth, you'll tap into that same youthful excitement.

## EXPERIMENTING WITH DESIGN

When you feel that neither your head nor your file folder can hold any more ideas, try sketching some of them on paper, using a scale of 1 inch = 1 foot (10 cm = 1 m), or larger if the scale will fit on the paper.

Identify design motifs that are particularly appealing to you and see if you can come up with spontaneous, simplified versions of them. Choose several and mix them in different scales. Be patient and spontaneous; you'll be amazed at how something that at first seems too simplified takes on a wonderful energy when executed in great colors. Narrow your

Opposite: Kathy Cooper, *Hawaiian Flowers and Stripes*, 5' x 7' (1.5 x 2.1 m), hand-painted acrylics
Photograph: Gordon Beall

Top: Kathy Cooper, *Abstract Roses and Checks*, 3' x 12' (.9 x 3.6 m), hand-painted acrylics
Photograph: Tom Cooper

Bottom: Constance Miller, *Salmon Pool*, 90" x 120" (2.3 x 3 m), sponged, stenciled, and hand-painted acrylics
Photograph: Michael Seidl

choices to a couple of design motifs and develop your ideas around them. (All those other great ideas can be saved for your next rug.) Add some dabs or squiggles of color as you go along to make your design pop or tone down a color for more subtlety; add a rule on top of an all-over design to contain it and suggest a border.

Whatever you do, don't labor over your initial design so excessively that you keep yourself from plunging into your project. And don't be afraid to follow your muse.

## TRANSFERRING YOUR DESIGN TO CANVAS

With a design sketch in hand and a floorcloth ready for surface decoration, you're set to transfer your ideas from paper to canvas.

Some artists jump right in and paint, others prefer to sketch the whole design first.

Begin by marking off the border. For marks that will be painted over, use a hard-lead, light pencil; for lines that might show or where you just need an approximation of the image for placement—such as a flowing free-hand ribbon running along the border—use chalk. (After the painting is finished and dry, wipe off any remaining chalk with a damp sponge.)

To translate a more complicated design from a small sketch to a large floorcloth, first draw a grid over your sketch. Then, using chalk, draw a larger but corresponding grid on the canvas. Transferring small sections at a time from your sketch to the appropriate squares on the rug will help you to keep the design in scale.

Another tried-and-true method for transferring a design is to create a "cartoon." Draw your design on a paper pattern cut the same size as the rug; lay the pattern on the canvas and punch

Top: Mary Moross, *Basket of Flowers*, 3' x 4' (.9 x 1.2 m), hand-painted acrylics
Photograph: Bill Miller

Bottom: Francie Anne Riley, *Autumn Leaves*, 21" x 34" (53.5 x 86.5 cm), sponge-stamped acrylics
Photograph: Putnam Photographic Laboratory

through the paper with a pencil, leaving marks on the canvas at strategic points to create a dotted outline on the canvas.

If you feel uncomfortable sketching freehand, images can be "borrowed" from a book or magazine and enlarged on a copier until they're the appropriate size. Such patterns can be transferred to the canvas by one of the above methods or used to make a stencil or block print.

Finally, there are a number of ways to add designs that don't require drawing. Simple checkerboards and other historic designs use only a ruler to create various-sized blocks. Block printing, stenciling, sponging, combing, photo transfer, and collage are some of the many other surface design techniques that

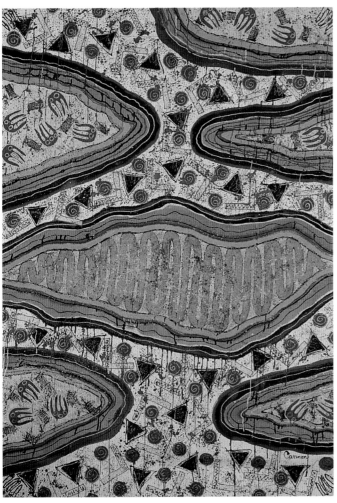

Top: S. Carter Keffury, *Gomorrah*, 6' x 9' (1.8 x 2.7 m), hand-painted acrylics
Photograph: Scott Porter

Bottom left: Carmon Slater, *DM II*, 60" x 83" (1.5 x 2.1 m), hand-painted pigments
Photograph: Pete Krumhardt

Bottom right: Sue Bleyaert, *Hay Lake*, 2' x 3' (61 x 91.5 cm), hand-painted latex

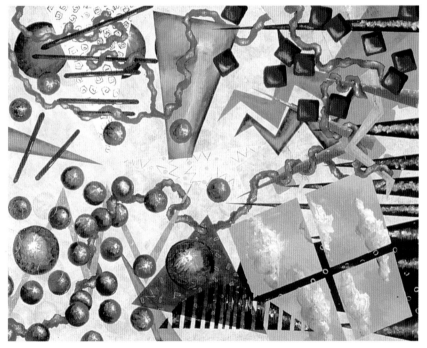

Top: Callahan McDonough, *Abstract*, 42" x 48"
(1 x 1.2 m), hand-painted acrylics
Photograph: Evan Bracken

Bottom: Marci Forbes, *Untitled*, 5' x 6' (1.5 x 1.8 m),
hand-painted acrylics
Photograph: Doug Cox

Right: Pomona Shea, *Abstract*, 2' x 8' (.6 x 2.4 m),
hand-painted acrylics
Photograph: Evan Bracken

can be used for decorating rugs. Just because you can't draw doesn't mean that you can't make a great floorcloth.

## COMPUTER PROGRAMS AND DESIGN

Until recently, the primary tools for designing floorcloths have been pencils, colored pencils, markers, and paint. Although a sketch never looks exactly like the floorcloth itself, it has been as close as anyone could get. If an artist is working with clients, photographs of existing floorcloths and sample swatches also can be used as backup information.

Then along came computers and their magical "paint programs." Today, a simple stylus can be used on an electronic drawing tablet just as if it were a pencil on a sketch pad. The results

Top: Laura Rogers, *Wildlife*, 3' x 5' (.9 x 1.5 m), hand-painted acrylics
Photograph: Chandler McKaig

Bottom left: S. Carter Keffury, *Lav*, 6' x 9' (1.8 x 2.7 m), hand-painted acrylics
Photograph: Scott Porter

Bottom right: Hilary Law, *Fork and Spoon*, 3' x 5' (.9 x 1.5 m), hand-painted acrylics and latex
Photograph: David Caras

are exciting. By writing with the stylus on the tablet, images are drawn directly into the computer, where there are infinite possibilities for variation and manipulation: motifs can be enlarged, shrunk, flipped, distorted, multiplied, and stored for use in other projects. An endless palette of colors can be added and taken away. Various "tools" can be designated to make the design look as if it's been sponged, stenciled, drawn freehand, brushed, or washed. In other words, the "sketched" design can take on the feel of an actual rug, allowing the artist to experiment with endless options before committing to canvas.

The computer unleashes creativity in a way having to draw and redraw an idea never could. Becoming proficient at any computer program takes practice, of course; but the computer ultimately saves time and expands options. Designs can be viewed at different stages and with different levels of detail, providing you with additional control over the finished product — and moving floorcloth design to a whole new level.

## FLOORCLOTH DESIGN CHECKLIST

~ Location

~ Use

~ Size Considerations

~ Measurements

~ Accent or Accessory?

~ Design Motifs

~ Border/Placement of Design

~ Colors

Top: Heather Allen, *830 Fogg*, 50" x 81" (1.3 x 2 m), hand-applied and silk-screened textile inks on industrial felt and canvas webbing
Photograph: John Lucas

Bottom: Barbara Benson, *Fall Leaf Mix*, 2' x 3' (61 x 91.5 cm), silk-screened textile paints and acrylics
Photograph: Thuss Photography

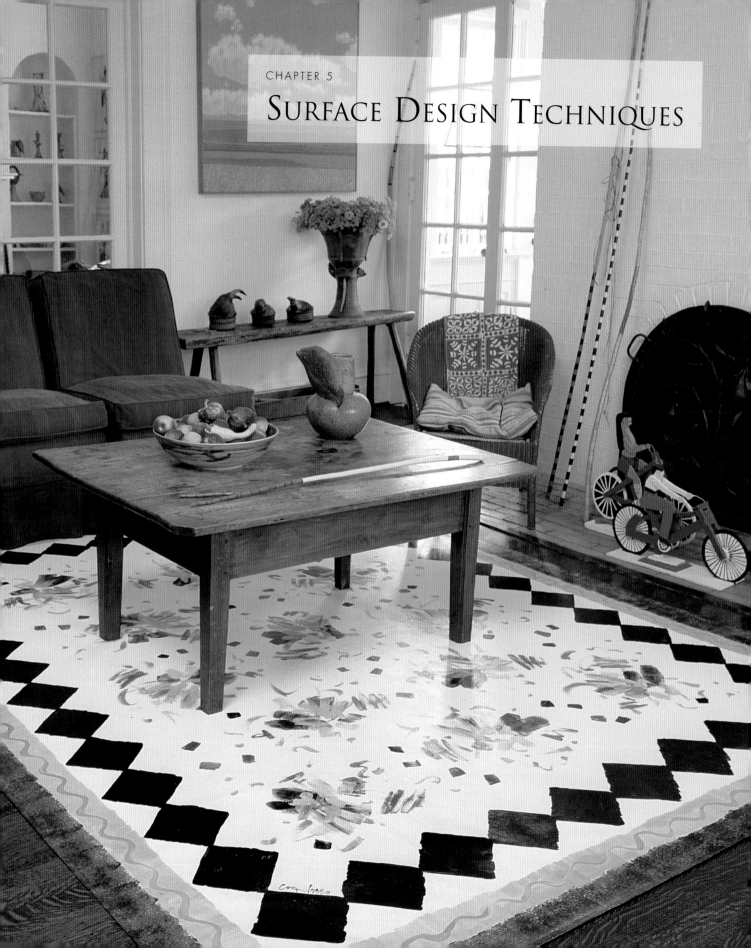

# CHAPTER 5

# SURFACE DESIGN TECHNIQUES

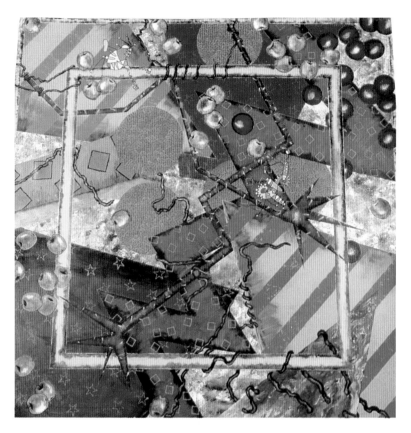

THERE ARE NUMEROUS WAYS to decorate your floorcloth — techniques suited to every interest and artistic ability. Nearly two dozen are described in this chapter. Many of these techniques build on information elsewhere in this book and on each other. They can be used singly or in combination.

The techniques described here are intended to be applied to a canvas that has already been primed and painted with two coats of background color. The background color used in the photographed examples is noted for each technique and has been chosen to enhance the technique used on top of it. When adapting these techniques for your own designs, be aware of how any color you choose will affect the colors or designs applied on top.

Several techniques described here (such as photo silkscreen, photo collage, and photo transfer) call for borrowing and enlarging images from printed sources. Keep in mind that it's a violation of copyright laws to copy and use copyrighted text, photos, or illustrations for other than personal use.

Previous page: Kathy Cooper, *Diagonal Checks with Confetti Center*, 7' x 9' (2.1 x 2.7 m), hand-painted and sponged acrylics
Photograph: Gary Warnimont

Top: Marci Forbes, *Untitled*, 4' x 4' (1.2 x 1.2 m), hand-painted acrylics
Photograph: Doug Cox

Bottom: Joan Weissman, *Untitled*, 4' x 6' (1.2 x 1.5 m), hand-painted latex
Photograph: Robert Reck

# SPONGE PAINTING

## BACKGROUND SPONGE WORK

### TOOLS
Natural (sea) or other sponge

Paint tray

### MATERIALS
Latex paint in various colors

Paint conditioner

### BACKGROUND
Yellow wash over white latex

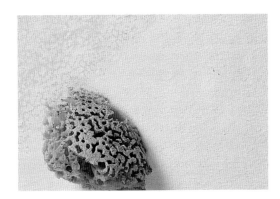

Pour some paint into a flat container, such as a plastic meat tray. Dip a moistened and wrung-out sponge into the paint, scrape off the excess on the edge of the tray, and test the effect by sponging on a scrap of paper or canvas. Lightly dab the sponge across the canvas, working in one direction and dipping the sponge in the paint as necessary. Notice that the position of the sponge, the direction you work, and the amount of paint are reflected in the pattern created.

Top: Susan Papa, *Untitled*, 3' x 5' (.9 x 1.5 m), sponged, stenciled, and stamped acrylics
Photograph: Eric Norbom

Bottom: Susan Papa, *Untitled*, 3' x 5' (.9 x 1.5 m), sponged, stenciled, and stamped acrylics
Photograph: Eric Norbom

For a softened or blended effect and added dimension, sponge on a second layer of another color that is relatively close in value to the first. Randomly dab the second color over the first to create a natural blend.

If your background color is a low-sheen paint (one that stays workable longer), another technique to soften the sponged effect is to dab a balled up piece of damp cheesecloth over the still-wet paint to remove some of the sponged layer.

Various sponges can be used to create different effects; those shown are (from left to right) a "picked" foam roller, a cellulose sponge, and a natural sponge. A picked foam roller is a tool used in the theater to add drama and overhead shadowing. It's made by randomly picking chunks of foam from the roller until the surface resembles Swiss cheese. The colors shown here are olive green over dark forest green, rust red over washed green, apple green over lavender, and white over taupe.

Susan Papa, *Untitled*, 3' x 5' (.9 x 1.5 m), sponged, stenciled, and stamped acrylics
Photograph: Eric Norbom

## SPONGE MOSAIC

### TOOLS
Small sponges (foam or cellulose) cut into ½"
(1.5 cm) and smaller shapes

Tracing paper

Plastic ice cube tray

### MATERIALS
Latex paints in "tile" colors

### BACKGROUND
Latex paint in gray "grout" color

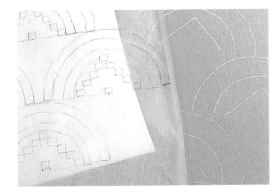

Sketch your design full size on a piece of tracing paper and punch holes at strategic points with a hard-lead pencil to transfer the pattern to the canvas. To make the design more visible on the grout-colored canvas, connect the pencil dots with chalk. Alternatively, use a grid to transfer detailed designs (see page 62).

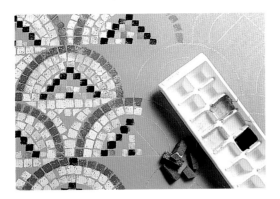

Cut a sponge into small squares that correspond to the "tiles" of your mosaic. Fill an ice cube tray with six or more colors that are similar to those of natural stone. Proceed to stamp in your tiles, working first along the outline of your design and leaving a slight space between squares to simulate grout. Mimic the natural variations in stone by adding a bit of a second color to the edge or corner of an already-dipped sponge.

Continue filling in the design by dipping sponges in various colors and stamping them in an orderly fashion over the design. To fill any remaining odd-sized spaces, cut additional sponges into triangles and other appropriate shapes.

Artist assist: Mary Moross

Mary Moross, *Royal Ducks*,
28" x 46" (.7 x 1.1 m),
mosaic sponge-painted latex
Photograph: Gerin Choinere

# PAINTING TECHNIQUES

## BRUSH WORK

### TOOLS
1½" (4 cm) flat bristle brush

1" (2.5 cm) flat bristle brush

Medium soft round (#6) brush

1" (2.5 cm) foam brush

### MATERIALS
Acrylic or latex paints in various colors

Matte medium or paint conditioner

### BACKGROUND
White latex

Brushes come in a wide range of sizes, and different types can be used to create a variety of painting effects. Simple house-painting brushes are suitable for many functions, including painting large areas of color with latex paint. Foam brushes are inexpensive tools for decorative painting and can be thrown away after your project is complete. Artist's brushes come in round or flat shapes, with stiff or floppy bristles. Among the most popular are soft rounds, which are good for detail painting and making thick or thin lines. Liner brushes are long, fine-pointed round brushes that produce long, continuous lines. Bright bristle brushes are similar to flat bristle brushes but have shorter hairs. Brights are suitable for short or long strokes, and flats are good for dry brush

Top: Cristina Acosta, *Leaves with Stripe*, 3' x 5' (.9 x 1.5 m), hand-painted acrylics
Photograph: Loren Irving

Center: Joan Weissman, *Untitled*, 42" x 60" (1.1 x 1.5 m), hand-painted latex
Photograph: Robert Reck

Bottom: Fran Rubinstein, *Canyon Lands*, 4' x 4' (1.2 x 1.2 m), hand-painted acrylics
Photograph: Bill Lemke

Top: Sue Bleyaert, *The Maple*, 30" x 60" (.8 x 1.5 m), hand-painted latex

Bottom: Hilary Law, *Spilarama*, 3' x 5' (.9 x 1.5 m), hand-painted acrylics and latex

Photograph: David Caras

mixing and painting larger areas. Choose whichever brushes feel most comfortable to you; many artists use a few favorites over and over, no matter what the painting task.

Match the brush and the effect you wish to create by adjusting the viscosity of your paint. For example, when working with a fine brush, dilute acrylic paint with a little water or add some paint conditioner to latex paint.

**Apple-green checks:** For a freehand checkerboard effect that doesn't require taping or a stencil, dip a foam brush in latex paint and work in quick, short strokes.

**Pink swirls and flourishes:** A small round brush produces controlled detail work and a fluid drawing effect.

**Yellow ribbon:** A medium-width ribbon effect is produced with a 1-inch (2.5 cm) flat

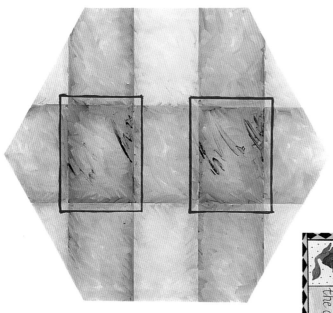

brush by rotating the brush and alternating heavy and light pressure.

**Green textured line:** A 2-inch (5 cm) brush is worked in short strokes perpendicular to the direction of the line, giving the line an informal ragged edge. (A brush stroked in the same direction as the line results in a smooth edge.) The brush is dipped first in green, then in white paint, and the colors are allowed to mix as the paint is applied, producing dark and light areas. Mixing paints on your brush as you work—dry brush mixing—adds more textural and visual interest to the surface than using a thoroughly mixed, opaque color.

Top: Alan Vaughn, *Untitled*, 3' x 3' (91.5 x 91.5 cm), hand-painted acrylics

Center: Brenda Shannon, *Hey Diddle Diddle*, 32" x 42" (81.5 x 106.5 cm), stenciled and hand-painted acrylics
Photograph: Tom Long

Bottom: Sue Bleyaert, *Stampede*, 2' x 4' (.6 x 1.2 m), hand-painted latex

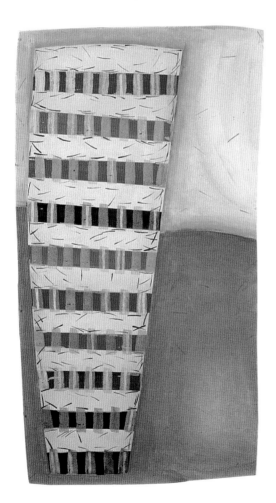

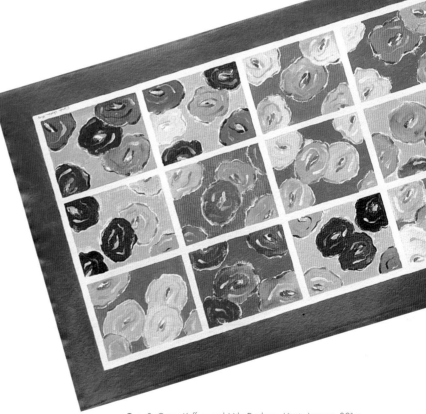

Top: S. Carter Keffury and Mila Dunham, *Virgin Lemons*, 30" x 72" (.8 x 1.8 m), hand-painted acrylics
Photograph: Scott Porter

Bottom left: Hilary Law, *Untitled*, 3' x 5' (.9 x 1.5 m), hand-painted acrylics and latex
Photograph: David Caras

Bottom right: Rhonda Kaplan, *Assorted Poppies*, 2' x 3' (61 x 91.5 cm), hand-painted latex
Photograph: Shelley Noble

## SQUEEZE-BOTTLE PAINTING

### TOOLS
Squeeze bottle
(small, with thin tip for control)

### MATERIALS
Airbrush paints or liquid acrylics

### BACKGROUND
White latex ground brushed over with a
purple glaze, then rubbed with cheesecloth
in a circular motion

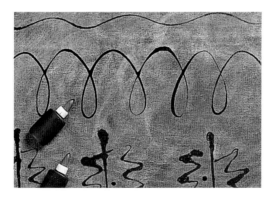

Squeeze bottles are useful for creating loose,
fluid lines. Fill the bottle with liquid paint and
squeeze as you move the bottle across the canvas, barely touching the surface. Both airbrush
paints and liquid acrylics, thinned with water,
are appropriate for this application. The paint
must be fluid enough to dry flat; thin and test
small amounts of paint on a scrap of canvas
until you achieve the desired fluidity.

Top: Constance Miller,
*In the Beginning II*, 36" x 58"
(.9 x 1.5 m), squeeze bottle,
acrylics
Photograph: Dave Curran

Bottom: Constance Miller,
*Carolina's Garden*, 30" x 84"
(.8 x  2.1 m), squeeze bottle,
acrylics
Photograph: Michael Seidl

## GLAZES & WASHES

### TOOLS
Cellulose sponge

Foam or flat bristle brush

Cheesecloth

### MATERIALS
Acrylic and latex paints

Matte medium

Paint conditioner

### BACKGROUND
Flat white latex

Technically, a *glaze* is a paint thinned with a clear medium, such as matte or gloss acrylic medium, paint conditioner, or acrylic varnish; a *wash* is a paint thinned with water. Both produce a thinned, translucent color, but their properties differ. A medium extends the drying time of paint, allowing it to be worked for a longer period; water speeds the drying time. The terms glaze and wash, however, are often used interchangeably.

Numerous glazed or washed effects can be produced using various tools to apply and texture the paint. Because acrylic paint dries quickly, work only a manageable area at a time so that the paint doesn't dry before you're finished.

**Green:** This glazed effect is created by wiping a darker color over a lighter background. Green acrylic paint, thinned with matte medium, is rubbed onto a white background with a damp cellulose sponge.

**Pink:** A translucent effect is created by thinning latex paint with paint conditioner, brushing it over a white base coat, and, while it's still wet, wiping it in a circular motion with a piece of cheesecloth. A rag, paper towel, or chamois cloth also could be used for removing and texturing paint in this manner.

**Tan:** An "antiqued" surface is created by using a natural sponge to wipe umber-toned paint, thinned with paint conditioner, over a white background.

Patricia Dreher, *Dark Landscape*, 60" x 114" (1.5 x 2.9 m), hand-painted with washed and glazed acrylics
Photograph: Valerie Massey

To create a "reverse" spatter paint effect,
sponge on an acrylic wash; then, while the
surface is still wet and workable, spatter it
lightly with water. While still damp, wipe
over the surface with the same paint-covered
sponge. The water drops will have softened
the paint beneath them, causing it to be
picked up and removed by the subsequent
sponging, thus producing random, colorless
spots across the surface.

## STANDARD GLAZE FORMULAS

### LATEX GLAZE

*2 parts latex paint*

*1 part water-based polyurethane*

*1 part water*

*Adjust the quantities of water and paint to achieve
the desired degree of translucency.*

### ACRYLIC GLAZE

*1 part acrylic paint*

*1 part acrylic varnish*

*1 part water*

### BILLY'S GOLD GLAZE

*1 part matte medium and gloss medium
(mixed 50-50)*

*Up to 1 part iridescent gold acrylic paint*

*Thin with water as needed; the resulting glaze
should be nearly transparent when dry.*

## GOLD LEAF EFFECT

### TOOLS
1" (2.5 cm) Flat bristle brush

### MATERIALS
Iridescent gold paint

Matte medium

Gloss medium

### BACKGROUND
Red iron oxide, thinned with matte medium, cross-hatched with a brush over white latex

Actual gold leaf is not compatible with acrylic varnishes and sealers, but a satisfactory reflective gold substitute can be achieved by using an acrylic gold glaze.

Gold is a good example of a paint used effectively as a glaze, since it requires the reflective qualities of the paint layer beneath it to enhance its metallic glint. Different background colors produce various effects, some more successful than others. Gold glaze applied over red iron oxide creates the traditional look of gold leaf; when used over an orange-yellow, the glaze simulates oriental gold. The same gold glaze over dark green produces an effect similar to bronze.

For the glaze itself, make a 50-50 mixture of matte medium and gloss medium in a jar, adding a generous amount of gold paint and thinning the mixture with a little water to make a workable consistency. Test the color and add gold paint as necessary until you achieve the desired effect. The glaze should be translucent when it goes on and may take several coats to build to the brilliance you want. *Note: gold glaze looks cloudy when it's applied, but it dries clear.*

Top: Brigid Finucane, *Phoenix Rising*, 25" x 62" (.6 x 1.5 m), hand-painted, sponged, and ragged acrylics and metallic paints

Bottom: Marjorie Atwood, detail, *Wild Things*, full size is 9' x 12' (2.7 x 3.6 m), gold leaf and oils
Photograph: Scott Miller

Top: Brigid Finucane, *Deco II*, 38" x 72" (1 x 1.8 m), stenciled and hand-painted acrylics and metallic paints

Bottom: Brigid Finucane, detail, *Deco II*

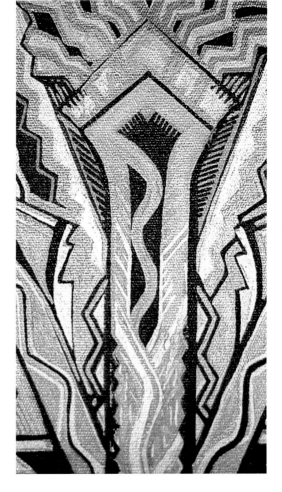

This gold leaf effect is created by layering several coats of gold glaze over red iron oxide, which has been brushed over the surface in free, cross-hatching strokes. The color of the gold itself will vary somewhat according to the brand of paint.

Artist assist: Billy McClain.

# COMBING

### TOOLS
Combing tool

Flat bristle or foam brush

### MATERIALS
Latex paint

Paint conditioner (if necessary)

### BACKGROUND
Medium sky blue low-sheen latex

Combing adds texture and visual interest to the canvas. To produce this pattern of energetic parallel lines, a combing tool is drawn through a layer of wet paint, allowing the base coat to show through. Using a low-sheen base coat prolongs the time during which the top coat is wet and workable, allowing more time for combing; adding paint conditioner to the paint extends working time even longer.

Working a small area at a time, brush a second, contrasting color on top of your (dry) low-sheen base coat; then, while it is still wet, draw the comb through the paint in smooth, continuous lines. The combing pattern can be varied by making the lines straight, wavy, cross-hatched, or basket weave—to name a few options.

Combing tools can be purchased in art supply stores or are easily homemade by cutting shallow V-shaped notches in a rubber scraper or in the straight edge of a plastic lid cut in half. Alternatively, substitute a screwdriver or pastry crimper.

Mary Moross, *Cranes*, 8' x 10' (2.4 3 m), combed, stenciled, and hand-painted latex

Photograph: Ileona Saurez

## MARBLING

### TOOLS

Spray bottle with water

Sea sponge

Paint tray

Wide China bristle brush

Chamois cloth

Cotton swab

Thin soft round or liner brush

### MATERIALS

Latex paints in colors similar to the following:

    Hooker's green

    Chrome oxide green

    Payne's gray

    White

Acrylic urethane varnish

### BACKGROUND

White latex

Marble is limestone that has been transformed over many years by the effects of heat and pressure. A realistic marble look can be

achieved by combining and manipulating several colors over a base coat. The colors shown here are simply suggestions; substitute others to suit your tastes and design parameters.

Before using this technique for the first time on a large area, practice on a small piece of primed canvas to get a sense of the properties of your materials.

Mix a thin green glaze by combining Hooker's green with chrome oxide green and adding an equal amount of acrylic varnish, thinning the glaze with water as needed. After pouring some of the glaze into a tray, rinse then wring out a sea sponge, dip it into the glaze, and blot the excess paint from the sponge. Lightly mist the surface to be painted

and apply the glaze in a random dabbing motion, loosely following an S-curve.

If the area is large, do small, irregular S-shaped portions at a time—no more than the equivalent of a 1- by 1-foot (30.5 x 30.5 cm) section. *Before* glazing the remainder of the canvas, proceed with the pouncing and subtracting techniques—described below—in the area you have just glazed. Then continue to mist, sponge, pounce, and subtract one section at a time until you've covered the entire surface. Lightly use the sponge to blend areas where color changes seem pronounced. Do not allow the paint to dry until you have completed the sequence of steps.

allowing the brush to linger on the paint. Keep your wrist moving from side to side to avoid creating a repeat pattern. To add additional random texture after pouncing, conservatively and quickly dab the still-wet surface with a clean, damp rag or chamois cloth.

While the paint is still workable (and misting as necessary to keep it so), add texture to the surface by "pouncing" it with a wide, dry China bristle brush. To pounce, hold the brush with your hand far up the handle and position the brush perpendicular to the surface; then tap it straight down and up quickly, without

While the glaze is still fluid (misting if necessary), begin "subtracting" some of the paint to create the veins. Wrap a piece of chamois around your finger or the tip of a brush handle and pull it through the glaze randomly, using a jerky motion and varying the pressure and direction of the tool. Remember, veins aren't lyrical, they're as jagged as lightning bolts—the result of violent, jarring geological events.

Top left: Pat Burgee, detail, *Delphic Sybil*
Photograph: Michael Houstle

Top right: Pat Burgee, *Delphic Sybil*, 41½" x 70" (1 x 1.8 m), marbled latex
Photograph: Michael Houstle

Pat Burgee, *Libyan Sybil*, 48"
x 70" (1.2 x 1.8 m), marbled
latex

Photograph: Michael Houstle

Mist the surface to awaken the previous painting and, working wet on wet, apply a second coat of green glaze that has been darkened with a small amount of Payne's gray. Working a small section at a time, dab the surface with the sponge, but this time covering it less completely; at times, sponge over the subtracted veins. Again pounce, varying the pressure and possibly the tools (a rag or chamois cloth also can be used to add texture). Use a damp cotton swab to refine and vary the shape and thickness of the veins here and there. Then allow the surface to dry.

Fill a thin soft round or liner brush with off-white glaze (white acrylic paint thinned with acrylic varnish). Beginning at different points from the original veins, pull the brush across the canvas in a jagged, random trail, varying the pressure and avoiding 45° angles. Allow the brush to run out of paint as you make each vein. Hold the brush at the end of the handle so that movement comes from the wrist and is less controlled. As each vein is completed, use a damp cotton swab to subtract paint and vary the vein's shape and thickness. Allow the paint to dry.

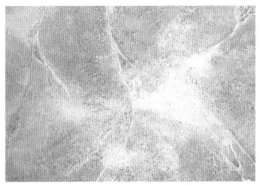

Sponge on a final, very light application of the original, undarkened green glaze, thinned considerably with acrylic varnish, and pounce. If desired, a light application of off-white glaze also can be added and pounced.

To achieve a realistic appearance, use colors that are relatively close in hue, intensity, or value. And don't be afraid to allow your sponge to pick up and deposit small bits of raw color. Expert marbling takes practice, but a folk art appearance can be achieved even by the beginner.

Artist assist: Pat Burgee.

Top: Sharon Lee, *Mosaic Madness*, 30" x 48" (.8 x 1.2 m), marbled oils
Photograph: Zave Smith

Bottom: Pat Burgee, *Untitled*, 41½" x 70" (1 x 1.8 m), marbled latex
Photograph: Michael Houstle

## Trompe l'Oeil

### Tools

Blue jay feather

Removable plastic adhesive

Light source

Hard-lead pencil

Bright bristle brush

Thin soft round or liner brush

### Materials

Flat white paint

Phthalo blue acrylic paint

Black acrylic paint

White acrylic paint

Matte medium

### Background

Sandy taupe, sponged and spattered with variations of the same color to achieve a faux stone finish

*Trompe l'oeil* is French for "trick the eye." In this technique, paint and shadowing are used to depict an object on a two-dimensional surface in such a way that it appears three dimensional. A blue jay feather is used in the example here, but any object can be substituted using the same principles.

Gently toss the feather onto the desired location on your canvas; adjust its position, right side up, and apply a small ball of plastic adhesive to the back to hold it in place. (Plastic adhesive is a taffylike product that is suitable for adhering three-dimensional objects temporarily to a background. It's available in office supply stores under several different names.) Position a light source to shine across the feather and create a strong shadow. Closing one eye and holding your head still, trace around the feather and the shadow with a pencil; be sure to connect the shadow to the feather at both ends.

Charles Goforth, *Sixth Floor,*
5' x 8' (1.5 x 2.4 m), hand-
painted acrylics with oil glaze
Photograph: Beth Phillips

Using a small bright bristle brush and flat white paint, fill in the outline of the feather with quick, short strokes. Follow the natural lines of the feather, brushing from the center shaft outward to simulate the grain.

Mix a small amount of a thin blue-gray glaze (phthalo blue plus a tiny bit of black and white). Apply over the white feather (except the tip), using the coloring of the actual feather as a guide. Add the appropriate markings with a thin soft round or liner brush. Finally, fill in the shadow with a thin gray glaze (black, white, and matte medium).

Artist assist: Pat Scheible.

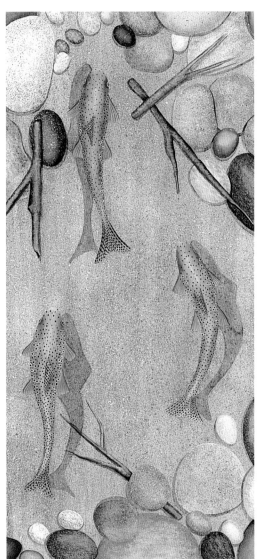

Top left: Evergreene Painting Studios, detail, *Untitled*, full size is 15' x 18' (4.6 x 5.5 m), hand-painted with oil glazes and paints
Photograph: Michael Imlay

Top right: Rebecca Sykes, *Egg Drop Soup*, 30" x 48" (.8 x 1.2 m), hand-painted acrylics
Photograph: Sanders Milens

Bottom: Maleesa Davis, *River Runs Through It*, 3' x 6' (.9 x 1.8 m), hand-painted acrylics

Top: Rebecca Sykes, *Leaves on Parade*, 41" x 65" (1 x 1.6 m), hand-painted acrylics
Photograph: Sanders Milens

Center: Liz Chase, *Institute Stairwell*, 52" x 108" (1.3 x 2.7 m), hand-painted acrylics
Photograph: Tenebrini

Bottom left: Jean Ebert, *Fish Pond*, 3' x 4' (.9 x 1.2 m), hand-painted latex and acrylics
Photograph: Eric Rauschenberg

Bottom right: Alan Vaughn, detail, *Ellis Island I*, full size is 4' x 6' (1.2 x 1.8 m), hand-painted acrylics

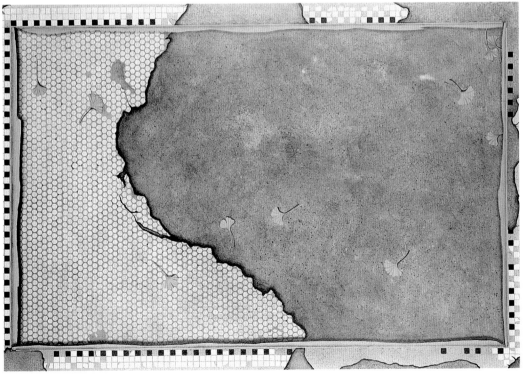

Top: Brenda Shannon, *Patio*,
2' x 4' (.6 x 1.2 m), hand-
painted and stenciled acrylics
with glaze
Photograph: Tom Long

Center: Rebecca Sykes,
*Carpe Diem*, 26" x 33" (66 x
84 cm), hand-painted acrylics
Photograph: Sanders Milens

Bottom: Charles Goforth,
*92nd Street Excavation*, 6' x
9' (1.8 x 2.7 m), hand-painted acrylics with oil glaze
Photograph: Beth Phillips

## AIRBRUSHING (NOT PICTURED)

### TOOLS

Small airbrush or large spray equipment

Air compressor

Tape or stencils

### MATERIALS

Liquid acrylic paint

Spray paints

Spray adhesive

Airbrushed paints or spray paints can be used to create fine details with quality lines, color uniformity, and no bleeding or streaking. The paint is applied over an area defined by masking tape, stencils, or other blocking methods.

Stencils can be cut from heavy acetate and coated on the back side with temporary spray adhesive. Allow the adhesive to dry, then press the stencil into place. Load the airbrush with properly thinned paint (beginning with one part water to two parts acrylic paint; your ratio may vary according to brand). Spray quickly and lightly. Do not attempt to achieve a uni-form color on the first pass; rather, apply several light coats, allowing the paint to dry between each. Shading can be achieved by subtly changing the tone and/or hue of the paint.

Excellent sandstone textures can be achieved with a commercial airbrush set improperly so that the paint spatters. Paint the canvas with an opaque grout color; then texture it by airbrush spattering with another color. Allow the airbrushed coat to dry. Now apply 1/4" (5 mm) masking tape to create grout lines and seal the tape by sponging it with grout-colored paint. Spatter the remaining surface with both a darker and a lighter color than the grout. Allow the paint to dry and remove the tape, revealing the original spattered surface as the grout lines.

When working with airborne paints, always use proper ventilation and breathing protection.

*Artist assist: Ben Jennings.*

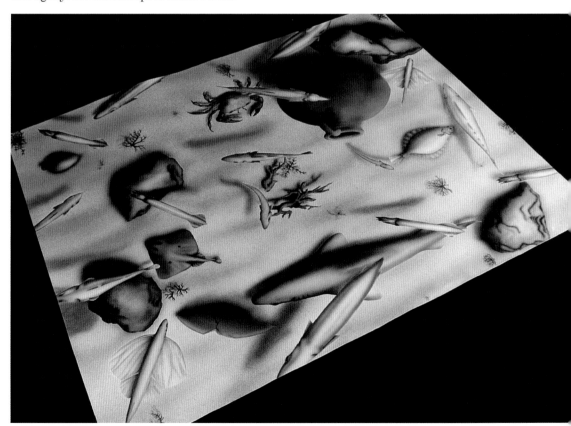

Gabriel Romeu, *Aegean Sea*, 4' x 5' (1.2 x 1.5 m), airbrushed and hand-painted acrylics

# PRINTED DESIGNS

## BASIC STENCIL WITH ADDED DETAILS

### TOOLS
Sketch or photocopy image

Acetate or other stencils

Cuticle scissors

Stencil brush

Painter's masking tape

Medium soft round brush

### MATERIALS
Acrylic paints in a variety of colors and washes

Matte medium

### BACKGROUND
White latex washed with orange-red paint, spattered with water, and wiped with a sponge (reverse spatter paint technique, see page 78)

Stenciling is an efficient and simple way to create images, and it doesn't require drawing skills to be effective. A stenciled design can be used alone or repetitively, several stencils can be combined to create a more complex image, and a stencil can serve as a base image that is embellished with hand-painted details, as shown in this example. Stencils can be filled in by painting, sponging, or spraying.

Cut a fish-shaped stencil from acetate, thin poster board, or stencil paper, and tape it in place. Fill it in by brushing with a stencil brush loaded with turquoise paint (phthalo green and white allowed to mix on the brush), working from the outside of the stencil to the center to avoid bleeding. For color variation, let several colors of paint mix during the painting process (dry brush mixing). Carefully remove the stencil and allow the paint to dry. Add the desired details to the flat stenciled image, using a medium soft round brush.

Pattern books, wallpaper, fabrics, and magazines are just a few potential sources for designs. If necessary, enlarge an image on a photocopy machine until it is the desired size.

Laura Curran, *Tea Time*, 4' x 6' (1.2 x 1.8 m), stenciled and hand-painted acrylics

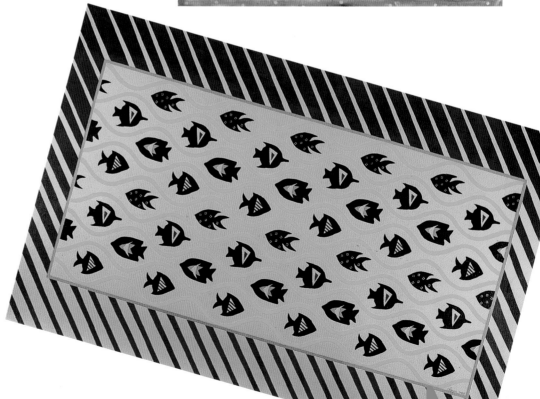

Top left: Roger Mudre, *English Tiles*, 2' x 3' (61 x 91.5 cm), stenciled acrylics
Photograph: Ty Hyon

Top right: Laura Curran, *Bath Time*, 5' x 7' (1.5 x 2.1 m), stenciled and hand-painted acrylics

Bottom: Laura Rogers, *Under the Sea*, 3' x 5' (.9 x 1.5 m), stenciled acrylics
Photograph: Chandler McKaig

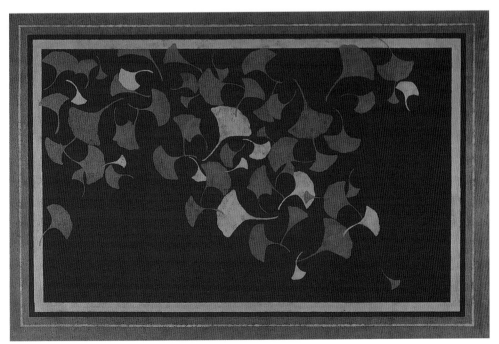

Top left: Kiki Farish and Carol Massenburg, *Jester*, 2' x 3' (61 x 91.5 cm), stenciled and glazed acrylics
Photograph: J. W. Photo Labs

Top right: Roger Mudre, *Victorian Floral*, 3' x 3' (91.5 x 91.5 cm), sponged and stenciled acrylics
Photograph: Ty Hyon

Bottom: Laura Gardner and Mary Moross, *Ginkgo*, 4' x 6' (1.2 x 1.8 m), stenciled latex and acrylics
Photograph: Gerin Choinere

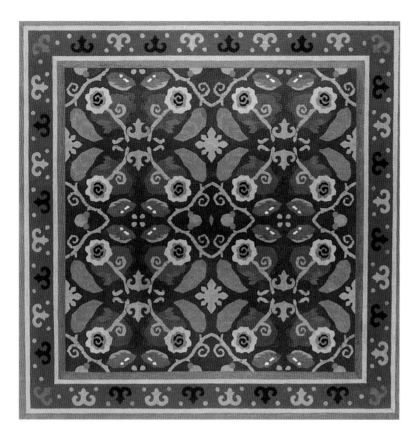

George Shinn, *Chimera*, 52"
x 52" (1.3 x 1.3 m), stenciled
mirror-image repeat acrylics
Photograph: Photocraft Lab

## MIRROR IMAGING & MULTIPLE STENCILS

### TOOLS
Acetate stencils

Masking tape

Hard-lead pencil

Stencil brush

Screening or texture (optional)

### MATERIALS
Acrylic or latex paints in various colors

Matte medium

### BACKGROUND
Navy blue acrylic or latex

A complex design can be created by rotating and flipping a single stencil in four quadrants around a center point. Four complementary images are created by printing the stencil right side up and upside down and from both the front and back. Historically, many carpet designs use this same mirroring motif principle.

One complete printing of this mirrored design covers a square 20 by 20 inches (51 x 51 cm) that is divided into four quadrants, each 10 by 10 inches (25.5 x 25.5 cm). Each quadrant is printed with the same three stencils, which are turned and flipped in successive quadrants, giving the impression of a much larger and more complex original stencil. This technique can be used once to create a center medallion or repeated across the canvas for a larger all-over design.

Begin by marking off the 20- by 20-inch (51 x 51 cm) grid—or multiples thereof—on your canvas, and dividing each square into four 10- by 10-inch (25.5 x 25.5 cm) quadrants.

Using the templates shown in the photo at left as guides, cut out the three stencils required for each quadrant. Then, before painting, use a pencil to trace the first stencil in all four quadrants (rotated and flipped as described below), being sure that a complete motif is formed where the stencils meet at the center point. This establishes the placement of your design.

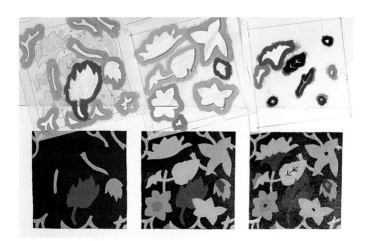

To paint, tape the first stencil in place in the upper left quadrant, positioning it so that the stem of the large red leaf faces down and curves to the right (the center). Following the color photos, brush on the appropriate colors. Different colors can be applied at the same time, as long as the images aren't touching each other. Allow the paint to dry.

Now use the same stencil to paint the diagonal (lower right) quadrant, rotating the stencil 180°, but painting from the same side of the acetate; the stem is now *above* the red leaf and curves to the *left*. Allow both canvas and stencil to dry.

To paint the two remaining quadrants, flip the stencil over and paint through it from the back. Position the stencil in the upper right quadrant so that the stem is *below* the red leaf, and curves to the left. Note that this quadrant forms the mirror image of the upper left quadrant. In the lower left quadrant, position the stencil with the stem *above* the leaf and curving toward the *right*; this quadrant is the mirror image of the lower right quadrant.

Repeat the procedure for the remaining stencils.

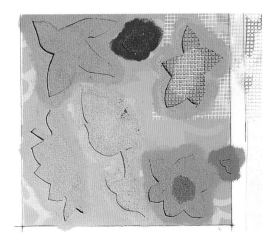

Textures, such as chicken wire, screening, or fabric, can be used in combination with stencils for added interest. Here a piece of screening is slipped under the stencil for the aqua blue flower and sponged over with taupe, giving the flower a cross-hatched texture.

Artist assist: George Shinn.

George Shinn, *Florabunda*, 52" × 52" (1.3 × 1.3 m), stenciled mirror-image repeat acrylics
Photograph: Photocraft Lab

## NEGATIVE IMAGE RESIST

### TOOLS
Adhesive paper or acetate & spray adhesive

Cuticle scissors

Flat bristle brush or sponge

### MATERIALS
Acrylic paint

Matte medium

### BACKGROUND
White latex

Top: Susan Kee, *Crazy Quilt*, 3' x 4' (.9 x 1.2 m), stenciled, dry-brushed latex with textured overlays and paper resist
Photograph: Dale Roddick

Bottom: Jan Harris, *Cranes*, 45" x 88" (1.1 x 2.2 m), stenciled acrylics and latex with adhesive paper resist
Photograph: Evan Bracken

In the techniques just described, stencils have been painted through to create a positive image; here a stencil is used to mask the background and create a negative image. The pattern causes the background to "resist" the color, hence the name.

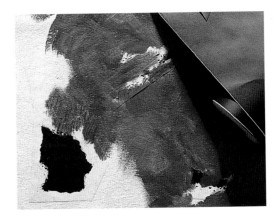

Transfer the image to a sheet of acetate or adhesive paper and cut out the pattern. Unlike stencils, image patterns cannot be reused, so cut out one for every image that will appear on the canvas. Adhere the pattern in place, sponging the edges with the background color to seal them. Brush, sponge, or spray a second color around the image, overlapping onto the pattern. Allow the paint to dry.

When the pattern is lifted off, the image is revealed in the background color. If desired, the image can be embellished using freehand painting or other methods.

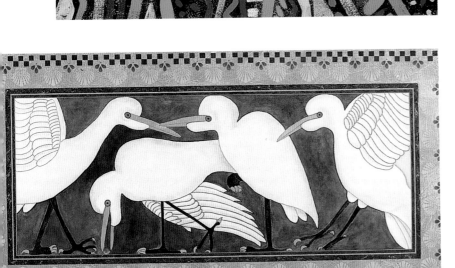

## MASKING TAPE BLOCK OUT

### TOOLS

Painter's blue masking tape

Sponge or stencil brush

### MATERIALS

Acrylic or latex paint for decoration

Matte medium

### BACKGROUND

Off-white latex

Painter's masking tape, used here to create a negative resist pattern, is an excellent way to create crisp, straight lines or, in this case, diagonal stripes. Painter's masking tape is distinguished from standard masking tape by the slower rate at which its adhesive cures, allowing the tape to remain in place for three to four days without leaving a sticky residue. It is particularly effective on fragile surfaces and will not remove paint that it has been taped over. Several colors and degrees of tackiness are available; the blue tape is recommended here.

Lay down the masking tape in the desired pattern. Press down tightly and seal the edges by sponging along the tape with the background color. Allow to dry. Paint in the unmasked area with a sponge or stencil brush. Allow to dry; then carefully remove the tape. *Hint: If paint bleeds under the tape, lightly scrape off the excess with a razor blade and touch up with background color if necessary.*

Top: Susan Kee, *Spring Inspiration*, 32" x 65" (.8 x 1.6 m), sponged, sprayed, stenciled, and ragged latex and acrylics with textured overlays and masking tape resist

Photograph: Dale Roddick

Bottom: Gary Mackender, *Untitled*, 54" x 78" (1.4 x 2 m), masking tape resist, acrylics

## BLOCK PRINTING

### TOOLS

Hard-lead pencil or chalk

Straightedge

Tracing paper

Carbon paper

Neoprene for cutting into block design

Mat knife

Wood block cut to size

Contact cement

Brayer

Glass or sheet of hard plastic, about 10" (25.5 cm) square

### MATERIALS

Cadmium red acrylic paint

Retarding agent

Matte medium

### BACKGROUND

Turner's yellow glaze over white latex

Block printing was one of the earliest methods used to make floorcloths in the 1700s. Then as now, it was favored for its ability to create quick, accurate designs. As with a stencil, a single block-printed image can be used repeatedly in the same or differing colors and positions, and can be combined with other blocks to form more intricate motifs.

Enlarge the selected image to fit your grid; then trace the image and transfer it to the neoprene surface. With a mat knife, outline and cut away the negative parts of the image (the areas that do *not* print). Cut just inside the drawn lines, as the paint will spread slightly when stamped.

Glue the neoprene pattern to the wood block with contact cement (do not use water-soluble glue, which will break down during cleanup). On the back of your wood block, draw two intersecting lines to mark the center of the block. You will align these lines with the grid lines on the canvas for precise placement of your design.

Using a hard-lead pencil, mark off the border, if desired, and divide the center area into a grid of squares equal in size to your wooden block. *Note: Rather than delineating the outside edges of your block, here the grid lines are placed to align with the intersecting marks drawn across the center back of your block.*

Mark the back of the block with a directional arrow to assist you in printing your pattern correctly. To keep printed lines straight on an all-over grid design, first stamp your center-most row in each direction; then continue printing until you've filled the entire field. Wash the block as necessary to prevent paint from building up or drying in the negative spaces. Wash all your tools promptly after use.

Artist assist: Virginia Kirsch.

Following the manufacturer's instructions, mix your printing color with retarding agent on the piece of glass or plastic. The retarding agent is similar to paint conditioner and will slow the paint's drying time, preventing it from drying on the glass or block before you have had time to print multiple blocks. Roll the brayer in the paint; then roll the paint onto the block, coating it completely but lightly. Before printing on your canvas, test the block print on a scrap of paper or primed canvas to get a feel for how much paint is needed to achieve the effect you desire.

Opposite: Constance Miller, *Wavy Green Runner*, 30" x 72" (.8 x 1.8 m), felt-stamped acrylics
Photograph: Michael Seidl

Below: George Shinn, *Aflorelle*, 52" x 52" (1.3 x 1.3 m), stenciled mirror-image repeat acrylics
Photograph: Photocraft Lab

## BLOCK PRINTING WITH VARIOUS MATERIALS AS STAMPS

### TOOLS
Wood blocks cut to size

Scissors

String

Felt

Cellulose sponges

Packing foam

Contact cement

### MATERIALS
White latex paint

### BACKGROUND
Medium blue flat latex

Printing blocks can be made simply by shaping a variety of materials and gluing them to a wood printing block. Here (left to right) packing foam, thin foam, sponges, rope, and felt have been cut and shaped to produce a variety of effects. Cut fruits, vegetables, or household implements—anything that can hold paint long enough to be stamped—also can be used. Print as described in the previous section, page 99.

Francie Anne Riley, *Floating Squares*, 21" x 34" (53.5 x 86.5 cm), stamp-printed acrylics
Photograph: Putnam Photographic Laboratory

## PHOTO SILK SCREEN

### TOOLS
Acetate image

Photo silk screen (done at silk screen shop)

Cellulose sponge

Plastic squeegee

### MATERIALS
Gray textile paint

Table salt

### BACKGROUND
Flat deep rose latex

Printing on canvas with a silk screen produces a precise, clearly defined image. This technique is effective for images too complex to be cut into a stencil and, like block printing and stenciling, is appropriate for creating multiple images. Textile paints rather than artist's acrylics are used because they dry more slowly and are less prone to dry prematurely on the screen. (For printing on unpainted canvas, felt, or other absorbent surfaces, add a pinch of table salt to the paint to break down the emulsion coating found on many textiles.)

Top: Barbara Benson, *Amish Series #2*, 3' x 4' (.9 x 1.2 m), silk-screened and hand-painted textile paints and acrylics
Photograph: Thuss Photography

Bottom: Barbara Benson, *Spring Woods*, 38" x 52" (1 x 1.3 m), silk-screened and sponged textile paints, mineral paints, and acrylics
Photograph: Thuss Photography

101

To create a silk screen, select your image and take it to a copy shop to be transferred onto acetate; then take the acetate image to a silk-screen shop to have it burned onto a screen. Alternately, you can burn the screen at home, using special sunlight-sensitive emulsions.

After planning the placement of the image, wipe the screen with a damp sponge to help the paint begin to flow through it. Spoon 2 or 3 tablespoons (30 or 45 ml) of textile paint onto the screen. The paint should be soft but not watery. Align the screen on the canvas and pull the plastic squeegee back and forth across the screen five or six times in each direction until the image on the screen is completely covered with paint.

Remove the screen carefully. You can reuse the screen immediately to print again in the same color as long as the screen doesn't touch the wet area you have just printed. To achieve a shadow effect, allow the first image to dry; then print the image again in another color, slightly offsetting it from the first printing.

Artist assist: Barbara Benson.

Top: Susan Robertson, *Night Moon*, 12" x 14" (30.5 x 35.5 cm), silk-screened water-based inks
Photograph: Mary Messick

Bottom: Susan Robertson, *Snake Ride*, 24" x 32" (61 x 81.5 cm), silk-screened water-based inks.
Photograph: Mary Messick

# PHOTO TRANSFER

### TOOLS
Photograph

Color copy on transfer paper
(done at color copy shop)

Cuticle scissors

Iron

### BACKGROUND
Flat white (or light-colored) latex

Photo transfer is a method for attaching realistic images to the canvas. The process requires special transfer paper, available at a copy shop or drafting supply store. Image sources can include real objects, fabrics, mementos, and family photos, making this technique a wonderful way to create a scrapbook-type theme rug to remember a special event, such as a birth, prom, or wedding. The transfers must be applied to a smooth painted surface that isn't too glossy; because the background paint reflects through an image, it also should be light in color. Applying images directly on gesso or on flat white wall paint is usually best.

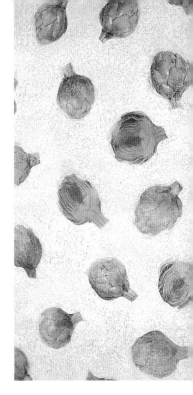

single sheet, since you will cut them apart before applying them to the canvas.

Use cuticle scissors to cut the images from the transfer sheet. Working on an ironing board, position one of the images face down on the canvas and, with a preheated iron set to the hottest setting, press straight down on the back of the transfer for approximately 15 seconds. Be aware of the effect of the iron on the painted canvas; try not to move the iron, as it can create scuff marks on the canvas. Remove the iron and, while the transfer is still hot, slowly peel off the paper backing, beginning at one corner. If the backing resists, continue to reheat and peel until the transfer paper is completely removed.

If desired, use paint on a liner brush to touch up the transferred images or background, add missing information, or enhance the design.

The transfer becomes a permanent part of the rug, similar to a design that is applied to a T-shirt, and it will be protected by the subsequent coats of sealer.

Artist assist: Laurinda Stockwell.

Top: Laurinda Stockwell, detail, *Artichoke*, full size is 5' x 7' (1.5 x 2.1 m), photo transfer, acrylics

Bottom: Laurinda Stockwell, *Water*, 4' x 5' (1.2 x 1.5 m), photo transfer, acrylics

Take the selected images to a copy shop and have them color copied onto iron-on transfer paper (the same process used to make T-shirt transfers). Transfer paper looks like color copy paper and runs through a copying machine the same way. Brands differ, so you may need to try a few to find the one that works best for you. Several small images can be copied onto a

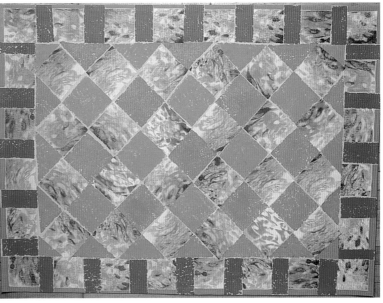

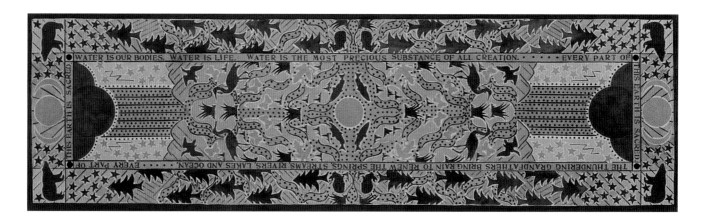

## RUBBER STAMP PRINTING

### TOOLS
Rubber stamps

Paint tray

Brayer (optional)

### MATERIALS
Acrylic paints in various colors

Matte medium

### BACKGROUND
Khaki glaze rubbed with cheesecloth over white latex

Top: Constance Miller, *Water Is Life II*, 2½" x 8½' (.8 x 2.6 m), rubber-stamped and stenciled acrylics.

Bottom: Constance Miller, *The Four Directions*, 7' (2.1 m) diameter, rubber-stamped and stenciled acrylics

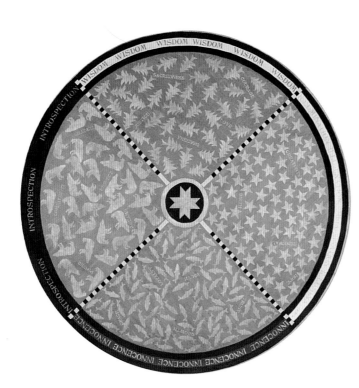

Store-bought rubber stamps offer an easy way to create repetitive images. Children's stores, art stores, gift and specialty shops, stationery stores, and catalogs are all likely sources of interesting stamps. Alternatively, you can create your own rubber stamps (see page 100). The relatively small size of most commercial stamps makes them appropriate for repeat border images, smaller rugs, or as small, complementary motifs used in combination with larger images.

Load a small amount of color onto a flat tray, such as a plastic meat tray. Dip the selected stamp into the paint to cover the rubber lightly with paint. Alternately, use a brayer to roll a thin layer of paint on the stamp. Be careful not to fill in the negative spaces of the stamp with paint. Test the stamp on some scrap paper or fabric; then stamp as desired.

Because acrylic paints dry quickly, it's advisable to stamp one color at a time and to clean the stamp promptly after use.

# OTHER TECHNIQUES

## HOLE PUNCH

### TOOLS
Clamps

Drill

Cut nail

Darning needle

### MATERIALS
Dyed cord

### BACKGROUND
Off-white latex

For variety and textural interest, floorcloth canvas can be punched, producing an effect similar to tin punching, or it can be punched and laced.

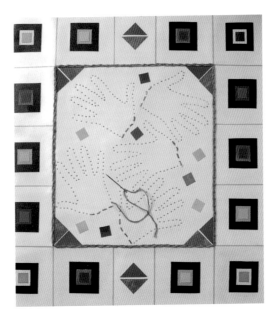

Leave the holes as is or finish the design by sewing in and out of the holes with a running stitch or an embroidery stitch.

Artist assist: Joyce Barker-Schwartz.

Joyce Barker-Schwartz, *Fire Flower II*, 6' x 7' (1.8 x 2.1 m), hand-painted acrylics and woven canvas
Photograph: Karen Mauch

Sketch your design and transfer it to the canvas using carbon paper (or see page 62 for other transfer methods). Secure the canvas, design side up, firmly and tightly to the work surface using clamps. Drill holes every ¼ to ½ inch (.5 to 1.5 cm) with an electric drill fitted with a cut nail. (A regular drill bit will catch and twist the fabric.)

## HOLE PUNCH HEM BINDING (NOT PICTURED)

### TOOLS
Electric drill

10 sheetrock screws

1" x ½" x 7" (2.5 x 1.5 x 18 cm) piece of hardwood

1" x ½" x 13" (2.5 x 1.5 x 33 cm) piece of hardwood

Wood glue

Hard-lead pencil

Hammer

Darning needle

Dual-duty (carpet) thread

An alternate use for punching and sewing is to create a decorative blanket-stitched hem. Complete your floorcloth through the surface design stage, taking into consideration that approximately ½ inch (1.5 cm) of the edge of your canvas will be covered with the blanket stitch.

Create a punch tool by drilling 10 small holes ½ inch (1.5 cm) apart through the 7-inch (18 cm) piece of hardwood. Into these holes, screw 10 sheetrock screws until their tips are poking through the underside and their heads are snug against the wooden strip. Glue the 13-inch (33 cm) piece of wood on top of the first, covering the screw heads and creating a 3-inch (7.5 cm) handle on either end of the tool.

Working on the painted side of your floorcloth, use a ruler and chalk or hard-lead pencil to make a continuous line around the perimeter of the canvas about ½ inch (1.5 cm) in from the edge. To make the holes for the thread, align the screw tips of your punch tool on the line you have drawn and tap the top of the wood handle with a hammer until the screws punch through the canvas. Continue using the punch tool to create equidistant holes around the perimeter of the canvas.

Finish the rug, using a darning needle and dual-duty thread to sew a blanket stitch around the edge. The thread will be protected by the subsequent coats of sealer applied to your floorcloth.

Artist assist: Pomona Shea.

Top: Pomona Shea, *Abstract*, 2' x 3' (61 x 91.5 cm), hand-painted acrylics
Photograph: Evan Bracken

Bottom: Pomona Shea, *Abstract*, 42" x 84" (1.1 x 2.1 m), hand-painted acrylics
Photograph: Evan Bracken

# COLLAGE

### TOOLS
Scissors

Hake brush (a Chinese collage brush, pronounced "hockey")

### MATERIALS
Decals, fabric, or other thin collage elements

Gel medium

Acrylic gloss medium and varnish

Acrylic matte medium and varnish

### BACKGROUND
Periwinkle blue latex

Collage can be used to apply decals, color photocopies, fabric, or other flat elements to the canvas surface. Like the photo transfer technique, it's appropriate for creating theme rugs or floorcloths to commemorate special occasions.

Chinese hake brushes are available at art supply stores and can be used for painting washes of color over broad areas as well as for applying collage elements to your canvas.

Make a collage "glue" mixture using approximately 1 cup (240 ml) each of gel medium, gloss medium, and matte medium, and ½ cup (120 ml) of water. Using the hake brush, apply a thin coat of collage glue to the back surface of the collage item and apply a thinner coat of glue to the canvas where it will be attached. Place the collage element on the canvas, glue side down, and use the hake brush to squeegee the surface, removing any excess glue or trapped air bubbles. Work neatly and swiftly in a back-and-forth motion

and avoid going back over the collage element, which can cause clouding. When all elements are in place and thoroughly dry, apply an even coat of collage glue over the entire rug surface, beginning at one edge and working in one direction until the canvas is covered. Allow the canvas to dry for 24 hours before applying the finish coats of sealer.

Artist assist: Maryellen Murphy

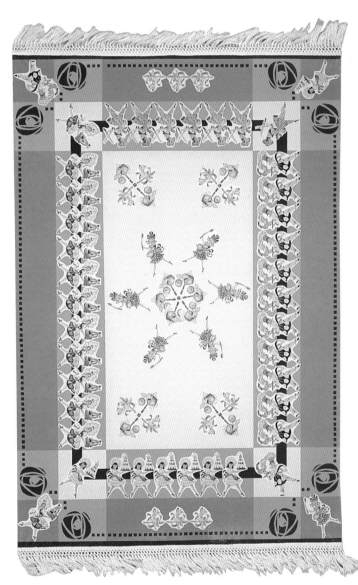

Maryellen Murphy, *Busby's Dancers*, 48" x 86" (1.2 x 2.2 m), hand-painted acrylics with 1940s decals and rug fringe

Photograph: Kate Cameron

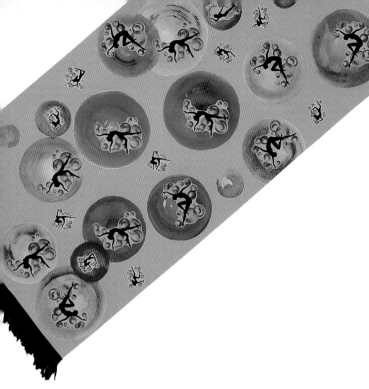

Top: Maryellen Murphy, *Deco Bubbles*, 36" x 86" (.9 x 2.2 m), hand-painted acrylics with 1940s decals and rug fringe
Photograph: Kate Cameron

Center: Sharon Lee, *Two Dogs*, 30" x 36" (.8 x 1.2 m), découpage with marbled oils and watercolor wood techniques
Photograph: Zave Smith

Bottom: Maryellen Murphy, *Fleur de Lis and Phoenix*, 36" x 73" (.9 x 1.8 m), marbled and hand-painted acrylics with phototransfers and rug fringe
Photograph: Kate Cameron

IF YOUR GOAL IS TO
CREATE a marvelous floor-
cloth with a well-tested
design, the following
projects will give you a
wide variety of looks
from which to choose.
Each is enhanced with a
number of decorative techniques
(explained in greater detail in chapter 5),
and the colors and size of the rug can be
varied to suit your personal taste and
interior design requirements.

The projects in this section begin with
an already primed and hemmed floorcloth,
painted with two coats of a background color
(specified in each project). To the finished size
of the rug, be sure to add sufficient additional
fabric to accommodate hemming and shrinkage. After completing the decorative steps
described for each project, remember to seal
and finish your rug as explained in chapter 3.

Previous page: Carmon Slater,
*fissures in the night sky,* 8' x
10' (2.4 x 3 m), hand-painted
with textile pigments
Photograph: Pete Krumhardt

This page: Various artists,
montage of project floorcloths.
Photographs: Evan Bracken

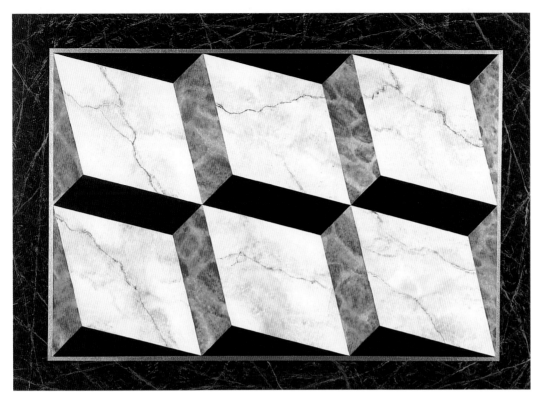

# SIX BOXES

*Design:* Sharon Lee

*Finished size:* 26" x 36" (66 x 91.5 cm)

*Photograph:* Zave Smith

This stylized series of six marbled, three-dimensional boxes is derived from illustrations originally published in British design books of the mid-1700s by Batty Langley and John Carwitham. The design combines an updated version of a classic pattern with an opportunity to try some simple stenciling and marbling techniques.

### BACKGROUND COLOR
Low-sheen white latex

### DESIGN COLORS
Black, white, burnt sienna, naphthol crimson, cadmium red, red iron oxide, raw umber, burnt umber, Hooker's green, yellow ochre, metallic copper

### TOOLS
Pencil, straightedge or ruler, painter's tape, 1" (2.5 cm) flat bristle brush, thin soft round or liner brush

### INSTRUCTIONS
**1.** Following the grid in figure 1, draw the design for the six stepped boxes on your canvas, setting the pattern within a 1-inch (2.5

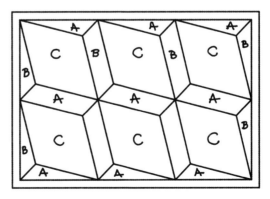

**Figure 1**

cm) inner frame and a 2-inch (5 cm) border. As shown in figure 2, tape off and paint black all sections marked A. Allow the paint to dry.

**2.** Tape off and paint all sections marked B with a river-stone marble glaze (figure 3). To make the glaze, begin with a clear glaze (acrylic varnish thinned as needed with water); then swirl in burnt sienna, naphthol crimson, cadmium red, red-iron oxide, raw umber, and Hooker's green, leaving the colors unmixed to create a mottled effect. Blot off the excess paint with a dry, crumpled rag; then let the surface dry.

**3.** Over the same B areas, float more clear glaze and add small, stone-shaped spots of color. Mix one of the colors from the river-stone marble glaze with clear glaze to create the tint, choosing whatever color you wish to be dominant. While the glaze is still wet, subtract a few veins by wrapping a rag around your finger or brush handle and dragging it through the glaze. Allow this to dry; then apply additional stone shapes in other colors.

**4.** Tape off and paint all sections marked C with a sienna marble glaze (figure 4). Begin with a white latex glaze (two parts white, one part polyurethane, one part water) applied over the surface; then add burnt sienna and yellow ochre right from the tubes, painting the acrylics into the glaze in irregular shapes of color. Again, soften the effect by dabbing with a rag and allow the surface to dry. With a thin soft round or liner brush and black glaze, add jagged lines to simulate veins. Lightly sponge with a slightly lighter version of the sienna marble glaze (add some white to the same mixture). Allow to dry.

**5.** Tape and paint the narrow 1-inch (2.5 cm) frame with metallic copper; allow to dry.

**6.** Tape and paint the 2-inch (5 cm) outer border with a tinos marble glaze—three layers of the same green glaze that is lightened each time with an increasing amount of white paint. The first layer of olive-green latex glaze is a mixture of green, dark brown, black, and white, all thinned with acrylic varnish and water. Apply the glaze and soften the effect with a rag. After allowing the surface to dry, apply a lighter shade of the same glaze and blot the excess with a rag. Allow to dry; then

apply a third still lighter version of the glaze, again softening it with a rag.

**7.** To complete the tinos marble border, draw random veins in black, thinned with a clear glaze if needed. Again, soften the effect with a rag.

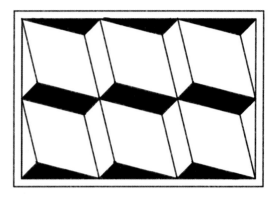

**Figure 2**

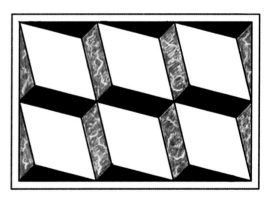

**Figure 3**

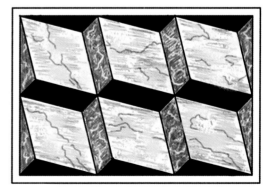

**Figure 4**

# FOREST FLOOR

*Design:* Francie Anne Riley

*Finished size:* 21" x 34" (53.5 x 86.5 cm)

*Photograph:* Putnam Photographic Laboratory

You'll feel as though you're walking in the woods with this informal, natural-looking floorcloth underfoot. The design incorporates washes, sponging, stamping, and masking tape techniques to create an impressionistic background with stylized tree leaves. Further interest is added by texturing the surface with a picked foam roller—a roller with chunks of foam randomly picked out until its surface resembles Swiss cheese.

**BACKGROUND COLOR**
Flat white latex

**DESIGN COLORS**
Chrome green, Hooker's green, burnt umber, cadmium red, metallic gold

**TOOLS**
Sea sponge, picked foam roller, four sponges cut into leaves of different shapes and sizes, two miscellaneous sponge shapes for border stamping, blue painter's masking tape, foam or wide flat bristle brush

### INSTRUCTIONS

**1.** Using the brush or sponge, wash the background with chrome green paint diluted with water; then, while the surface is still wet, sponge it lightly with a darker mixture of chrome green and Hooker's green. Let dry.

**2.** To simulate the feel of shadows from overhead trees, roll the canvas with the textured foam roller dipped in a brownish green wash (figure 1) made by combining the two greens with some burnt umber and diluting the mixture with water. Allow to dry.

**3.** As shown in figure 2, stamp the four leaf sponges randomly over the entire surface of the canvas. Allow some leaves to overlap naturally. Select one sponge for each color and stamp the leaves in burnt umber, chrome green, Hooker's green, and a mottled mixture of all three colors drizzled into a tray but not blended. Allow to dry.

**4.** Tape off a border 1½ inches (4 cm) wide and brush it with a mixture of burnt umber and red iron oxide. Don't be concerned if some of the leaves show through the border; they will add another element of interest to the finished design. Allow the paint to dry.

**5.** To give more texture to the border, sponge it randomly with one of the irregularly shaped sponges dipped in cadmium red. After allowing the red to dry, sponge again with another irregularly shaped sponge dipped in metallic gold (figure 3). Allow the border to dry thoroughly.

**6.** Accent the center area of the rug by stamping randomly with one of the leaf sponges dipped in metallic gold. Allow to dry.

**Figure 1**

**Figure 2**

**Figure 3**

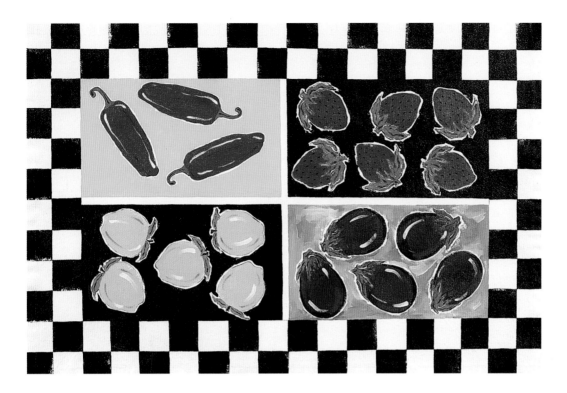

# VEGGIES & FRUIT

*Design:* Rhonda Kaplan

*Finished size:* 2' x 3' (61 x 91.5 cm)

*Photograph:* Evan Bracken

Unless you're a fast-food junkie, you'll love the appeal of this colorful grid of strawberries, chili peppers, eggplants, and apples—all wrapped in a snappy black-and-white checked border. The design combines traditional motifs with an updated format in techniques perfect for the person interested in trying his or her hand at a little painting and negative-resist stenciling.

### BACKGROUND COLOR
Flat white latex

### DESIGN COLORS
Black, white, cadmium red, cadmium yellow, chrome green, dioxazine purple, Hooker's green

### TOOLS
Hard-lead pencil, painter's tape, cardboard, adhesive paper, sponge, 2" (5 cm) foam brush, permanent markers, medium or fine soft round brush

### INSTRUCTIONS

**1.** Using a hard-lead pencil, create a 4-inch-wide (10 cm) border around the perimeter of the rug and mark it off into 2-inch squares. Divide the remaining center area into four equal quadrants, leaving a ½-inch (1.5 cm) margin between the four panels (figure 1).

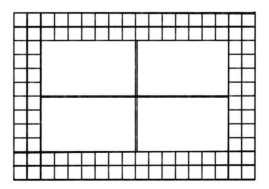

**Figure 1**

**2.** Create cardboard templates for the fruits and vegetables, cutting them slightly larger than you would like the final images. Trace them onto the adhesive paper and cut out the shapes. Arrange the fruits and vegetables in their respective panels; then remove the backing from the adhesive paper and press the shapes firmly in place.

**3.** Working on one quadrant at a time, tape around the outside of each panel, sealing the tape and self-stick templates by dabbing the edges with the background color; allow to dry. Paint the background of each panel its respective color—black for the strawberries and apples, yellow-orange for the peppers, and green for the eggplants (figure 2).

Alternatively, in place of solid-color backgrounds, you can create a watercolor effect for each quadrant by loosely blending different shades of a single color mixed with white. Allow each panel to dry before painting the next; then remove the last of the tape and all of the self-stick templates.

**4.** Using a paint pen or permanent marker, draw an outline within each fruit and vegetable shape, leaving a little white halo between the outlined image and the background color to set off the image (see figure 2).

**5.** Paint each fruit and vegetable in the appropriate color (figure 3).

**6.** Using a 2-inch (5 cm) foam brush, fill in alternate squares in the checkerboard grid (figure 4). For an irregular edge with a worn or weathered look, lift the foam brush occasionally toward the end of the stroke. Alternately, you can make the squares very precise by taping them off before painting.

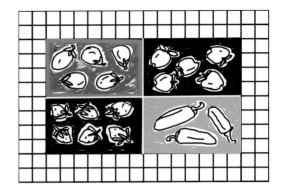

**Figure 2**

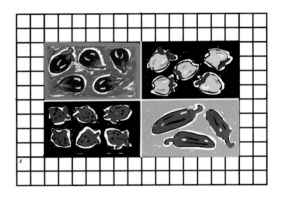

**Figure 3**

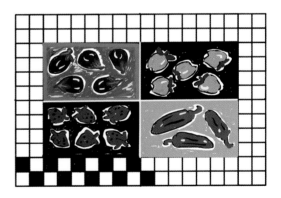

**Figure 4**

# GARDEN POND

*Design:* Kiki Farish

*Finished size:* 45" x 69" (114.5 x 175 cm)

*Photograph:* Evan Bracken

This lifelike carp pond will bring the outdoors right into your home. It's filled with ferns, butterflies, dragonflies, salamanders, and even a hidden fairy, all on a multiglazed surface. The design employs layers of color and a variety of painting techniques to achieve the effects of depth and reflecting light, both on and below the surface of the water.

### BACKGROUND COLOR
Low-sheen chartreuse latex

### DESIGN COLORS
Clay, steel blue, sage green, cadmium orange, red iron oxide, black, white, metallic copper, cobalt blue, ultramarine blue, Payne's gray, iridescent blue, chrome green, Hooker's green, metallic silver, cadmium yellow. (For better economy, use latex paints for the glazes and artist's acrylics for stenciling and details.)

### TOOLS
Acetate stencils for water border, frogs, carp, dragonflies, butterflies, ginkgo leaves, ferns, salamanders, and fairy; spray adhesive, stencil brush, thin soft round or liner brush, 1" (2.5 cm) foam or flat bristle brush, sea sponge, cheesecloth

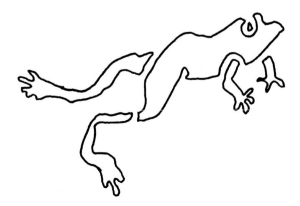

## INSTRUCTIONS

**1.** Using clay-colored latex paint straight from the can, sponge irregularly shaped rocks asymmetrically over the chartreuse background (figure 1). Allow to dry.

**2.** Following figure 1, add the carp, using the carp stencils and a stencil brush. Color them first with a red-orange mixture (cadmium orange, red iron oxide, and a little matte medium), and when this is dry, add a bit of metallic copper shading. Allow to dry.

**3.** To mute the vibrant colors of the carp and background, brush a steel-blue glaze (two parts steel-blue latex, one part acrylic varnish, and one part water) irregularly over the entire surface; then blot it with a damp cheesecloth to create a mottled but blended effect. Allow this to dry; then glaze again with sage green in the same manner as before. Allow the surface to dry completely.

**4.** For the water border, create several stencils that simulate sections of the irregularly shaped pond edge and can be laid down in varying combinations around the edge of the canvas. Cut other stencils to represent the various flora and fauna. Use spray adhesive to adhere the stencils to the surface while painting.

**5.** Working a section at a time, stencil the water border, first applying a coat of cobalt blue, then shading and blending with dark gray-blue and iridescent blue. Blend the colors with your brush to create a continuous watery edge (figure 2). Near the edges of the clay rocks, apply less of the opaque colors and more of the iridescent blue to achieve greater subtlety.

**6.** Stencil the frogs in green, highlighted with red iron oxide (figure 3); then brush on some iridescent blue within the water area, especially over the frogs and carp to create the impression that they're beneath the water's surface. Allow to dry.

**7.** The remaining stenciled images are meant to appear on the surface of the water or hovering just above it. Stencil hovering insects in black and, after allowing them to dry, add details with a soft round or liner brush and the appropriate colors. Stencil the ferns, layering lighter green over darker; paint the

ginkgo leaves chrome green, darkening an edge on each one to make them appear to float; add salamanders on the rocks, using greens and yellow; and place a subtle fairy in metallic silver in one corner.

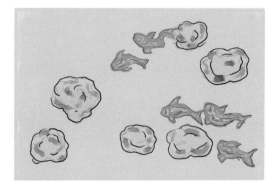

**Figure 1**

**Figure 2**

**Figure 3**

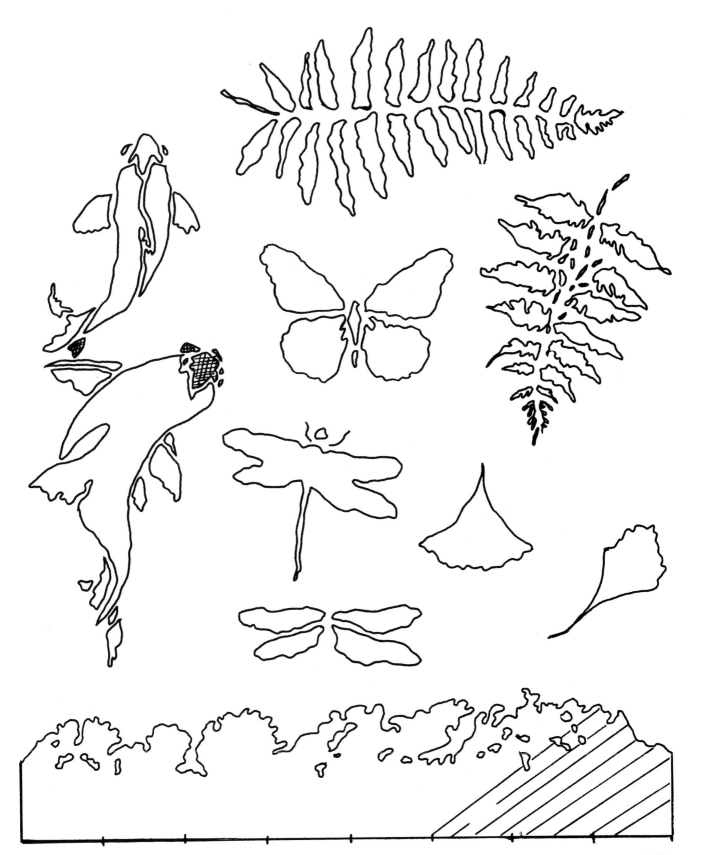

## PEACOCK

*Design:* Sue Hardy

*Finished size:* 2' x 3' (61 x 91.5 cm)

*Photograph:* Evan Bracken

This striking art deco peacock, stenciled in golds and copper on a black background, will add a dramatic accent to any room. The classical motif is updated with a surprisingly contemporary border, resulting in a complex design that makes use of advanced stencil-cutting techniques.

### BACKGROUND COLOR
Flat black latex

### DESIGN COLORS
Metallic gold, metallic copper, antique gold, metallic green, metallic blue, black

### TOOLS
Plastic stencil film, permanent marker, cuticle scissors or electric stencil-cutting knife, hard-lead pencil, compass or circle template, spray adhesive, stencil brush, flat bristle or foam brush, cheesecloth, painter's masking tape

### INSTRUCTIONS
**1.** Enlarge the design templates and transfer them with a permanent marker onto your stencil material. Cut out the stencils with cuticle scissors or with an electric stencil-cutting knife.

**2.** With a pencil, draw one line around the perimeter of your canvas 1 inch (2.5 cm) from the edge and another line 4 inches (10 cm) from the edge. Add a convex curve on each of the inside corners, using a compass or template (figure 1). Apply masking tape around the resulting 3-inch (7.5 cm) border and sponge the tape with background paint to seal it. Allow to dry.

**3.** Using a stencil brush, paint the border with gold paint and allow it to dry. Use a flat bristle or foam brush to paint over the gold with copper glaze, blotting the glaze with cheesecloth while still wet to create a mottled effect (see figure 1). Allow to dry.

**4.** Affix the large peacock stencil in position in the center, using tape and spray adhesive. Then fill in the stencil, using figure 2 and the photo as your guides. For the body and flowers, load the stencil brush, as needed, with metallic gold, antique gold, and copper, all thinned with matte medium. Use a mixture of metallic blue and metallic green for the "eyes" on the large feathers. Allow to dry. Cut a small, heart-shaped stencil and use this to apply a black center to each feather eye.

**5.** Stencil the feather border on the outermost edge, using gold and a mixture of metallic blue and green. Allow to dry.

**6.** Complete the 3-inch (7.5 cm) gold and copper inner border by stenciling the corner peacocks in black (figure 3). *Note: The narrow ends of the rug require only one peacock tail to be stenciled.*

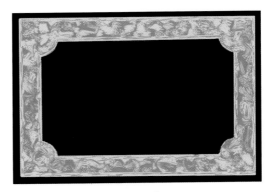

**Figure 1**

**Figure 2**

**Figure 3**

# GEOMETRICKS

*Design:* George Shinn

*Finished size:* 54" x 54" (137 x 137 cm)

*Photograph:* Photocraft Lab

This striking contemporary geometric design features a center medallion in a traditional nine-patch pattern and a border of triangles, squares, and intersecting lines. Although the finished piece looks very complex, it's easily accomplished in a series of steps, using painter's tape and stencils.

**BACKGROUND COLOR**
Russet orange latex

**DESIGN COLORS**
Hooker's green, black, white, cadmium red, cadmium yellow

**TOOLS**
Painter's masking tape, foam or flat bristle brush, acetate stencils for border and center, stencil brush

## INSTRUCTIONS

1. Run a line of 1-inch (2.5 cm) painter's tape around the outer perimeter of the canvas, masking off the outermost inch (2.5 cm). Tape off a 36-inch (91.5 cm) square exactly in the center and extend the tape in all four directions to the edges of the canvas so that you also create four small corner squares, each 7 by 7 inches (18 x 18 cm), and four side rectangles, each 7 by 36 inches (18 x 91.5 cm). (See figure 1.) To speed your painting later, mark a pencil line along the inside edge of the tape, forming the central 36-inch (91.5 cm) square.

2. Mix a pale beige by combining white paint with touches of yellow and black. Using a foam or flat bristle brush, paint the four corner squares and four rectangles beige. Allow to dry.

3. Following the photo and figure 1, tape off the 19- by 19-inch (48.5 x 48.5 cm) jagged center medallion. The medallion is composed of 13 4½-inch (11.5 cm) squares that are stacked in five rows set on the diagonal. Paint the medallion beige and allow it to dry.

4. Remove all the tape from the border and lay new tape to mask off the lines (now showing in the russet background color) created by the original tape. Use the pencil line as a guide to place your tape 1 inch (2.5 cm) inside the center square. Paint the resulting grid dark green, using a stencil brush for greater control.

5. Now remove the tape from the center medallion and tape just inside its outer edge to create a 1-inch (2.5 cm) border around the medallion. Paint the border dark green. Allow to dry.

6. As shown in figure 2, tape off a grid in the center medallion, extending the tape completely across the medallion to form 13 diagonal squares. Paint the appropriate lines green. As shown, add stripes to nine of the squares by masking out alternating strips of beige background and painting the spaces between them dark green. Allow to dry.

7. Mask and fill in the four unstriped squares in the center medallion and paint them dark red. Allow to dry.

**Figure 1**

**Figure 2**

**Figure 3**

**8.** In each corner square, tape off a 3-inch (7.5 cm) square box in the center and mark the inside edges of the tape with a pencil. Mask off the dark green grid lines in each corner and paint the square doughnut shapes red. Allow to dry.

**9.** Remove the tape from the corner boxes and apply new tape to create a 1-inch (2.5 cm) border around the beige centers, using the pencil lines to guide your placement of the tape. Paint the border dark green. Allow to dry.

**10.** Cut two stencils for the rectangular sections of the border, one for red, another for green. Each is 18 inches (45.5 cm) long and is printed twice in each rectangular panel—once right side up and once rotated 180° on center (figure 3). In one rectangular area, stencil the green left half first and allow it to dry; then rotate the stencil 180° and stencil it on the right half, leaving the far right stripes unpainted. Allow to dry.

**11.** Now stencil the red left side and allow it to dry. Rotate the stencil 180° and paint the far right red side.

**12.** Following the same sequence, complete the other three rectangles.

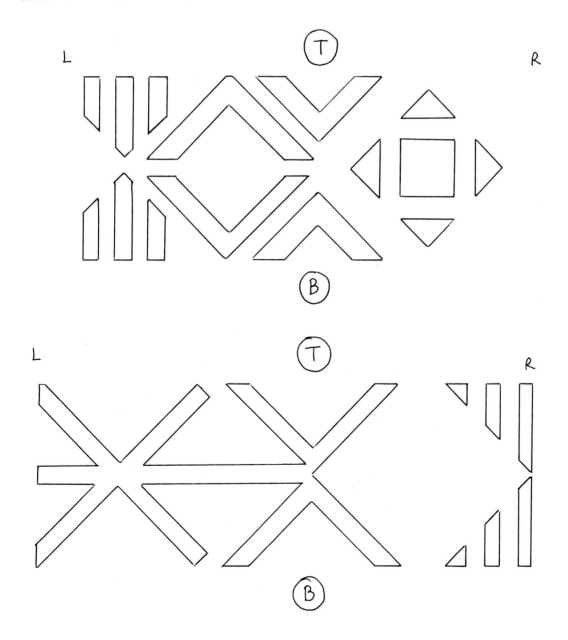

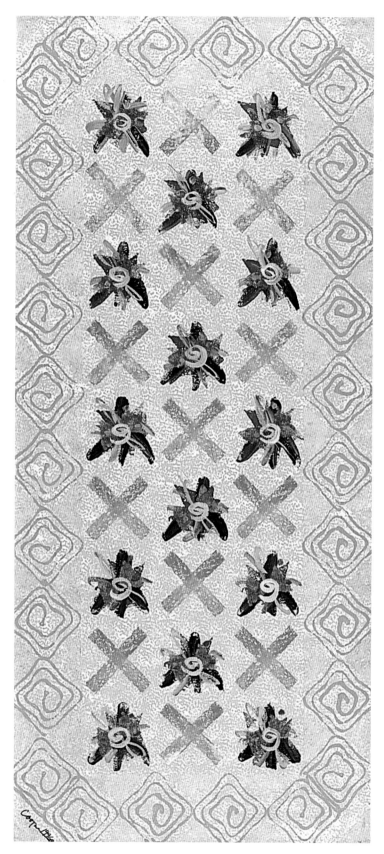

# SPONGE ROSE

*Design:* Kathy Cooper

*Finished size:* 30" x 66" (76 x 167.5 cm)

*Photograph:* Evan Bracken

This light-hearted, informal design consists of a sponge-printed and block-printed floral pattern on a sponged background. The impressionistic flowers are actually simple combinations of stamped triangles, a few swirls of the brush, and some dabs of paint.

## BACKGROUND COLOR
Taupe latex

## DESIGN COLORS
White, alizarin crimson, cadmium yellow, Hooker's green, phthalo green, cadmium orange, yellow ochre (latex), dioxazine purple, ultramarine blue

## TOOLS
Sponge, straightedge, chalk, block stamp (made from string glued on wooden block), small cut sponges, 1" (2.5 cm) flat bristle brush, medium (#6) soft round brush

## INSTRUCTIONS

**1.** Sponge white paint over the entire taupe background with a sea or cellulose sponge. Allow to dry. Using a straightedge and chalk, divide and mark the entire canvas into a grid of 6-inch (15 cm) blocks.

**2.** Use a large, triangular-shaped sponge approximately 6 inches (15 cm) wide along the base and 3 inches (7.5 cm) tall to print twice around the perimeter of the rug in a mottled mix of cadmium yellow, cadmium orange, and white. Print first with the wide base of the sponge facing the outer border of the inside field of 27 blocks; then stamp the sponge with the wide base against the outside hem edge (figure 1). Allow to dry.

**3.** In the border area that has been created between the yellow triangles, print the string-patterned block in yellow ochre latex, varying the direction of the block as you go (figure 2). Allow to dry.

**4.** Using the same large triangular sponge as in step 2, print two Hooker's green triangles to simulate leaves in alternate squares of the center field (figure 2).

**5.** Using a 1-inch (2.5 cm) flat brush, apply a mixture of white and phthalo green in short strokes emanating from the center of the leaves. Add smaller strokes in a similar manner with a medium round brush and allow to dry.

**6.** With a small triangular sponge dipped in a mottled combination of alizarin crimson and white, print pink flowers on top of the leaves. Add small swirling strokes around the flowers with the round brush (figure 3). Allow to dry.

**7.** Add a spiral made of cadmium yellow and white on the center of each flower and place lavender dots nearby, using a mixture of dioxazine purple and white.

**8.** Using the long, narrow edge of a large cellulose sponge, print sky-blue (ultramarine blue plus white) Xs in the empty squares of the center field.

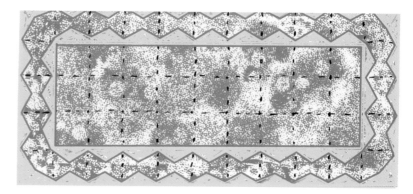

**Figure 1**

**Figure 2**

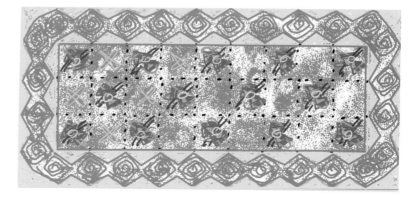

**Figure 3**

# SUNNY RUG

*Design:* Kathy Cooper

*Finished size:* 30" x 36" (76 x 91.5 cm)

*Photograph:* Evan Bracken

A floorcloth is a wonderful way to preserve artwork from a child's early years, and it makes a great gift for a young child, grandparents, or a special family friend. Here, simple hand-painting and combing techniques are combined with paint pens to embellish a child's drawing that is set within a brightly colored, playful border. This floorcloth will bring joy to any room!

**BACKGROUND COLOR**
Flat white latex

**DESIGN COLORS**
Cadmium orange, cadmium yellow, cadmium red, phthalo green, dioxazine purple, black, white

**TOOLS**
Hard-lead pencil, 1½ " (4 cm) and 1" (2.5 cm) flat bristle brushes, combing tool, medium soft round brush, painter's masking tape (optional), paint pens

## INSTRUCTIONS

**1.** Select one or more of your child's drawings for your design. When making your choice, look for bold and colorful graphic images that will be easy to recreate within the center field of the rug.

**2.** Mark an approximate 6-inch (15 cm) border in pencil, extending each line all the way to the edge and letting your lines be free and somewhat uneven, as if done by a child. Don't worry about accuracy; a wavy line will look more natural.

**3.** Leaving the corner squares unpainted, fill in the rest of the border by brushing on a mixture of cadmium orange, cadmium yellow, and white. Use the larger flat brush for even coverage. After this has dried, add a layer of cadmium red and comb through it while the paint is still wet (figure 1). Allow to dry.

**4.** Paint the corners turquoise, using a combination of phthalo green and white. (Mask the edges of the combed areas, if desired.) Allow to dry. In each corner, paint a cheerful sun, using the smaller flat brush and a mixture of cadmium yellow, cadmium orange, and white (figure 2).

**5.** In the center of the rug, pencil in the figures from your child's drawing or transfer the drawing, using one of the techniques on page 62 (figure 3). Before transferring them, the images may need to be enlarged to fit the space on your floorcloth.

**6.** Fill in the shapes with the appropriate colors, using a small round brush. Allow to dry. Using paint pens, outline the shapes and add smaller details, imitating a child's hand with your lines. Allow to dry.

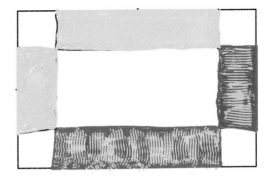

**Figure 1**

**Figure 2**

**Figure 3**

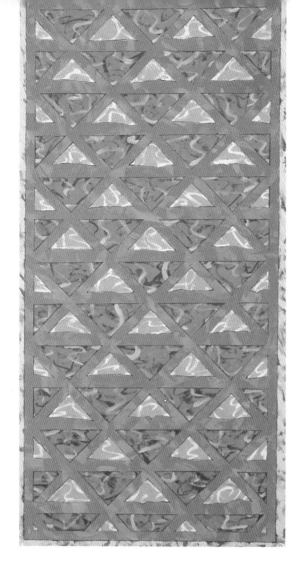

Top left: Gary Mackender, *Untitled*, 36" x 78" (.9 x 2 m), masking tape resist, acrylics

Top right: Carmon Slater, *Sanabel*, 59" x 79" (1.5 x 2 m), applied pigments
Photograph: Pete Krumhardt

Bottom: Susan Kee, *Self-Portrait Crazy Quilt*, 41" x 66" (1 x 1.7 m), stenciled, dry-brushed latex with textured overlays and paper resist
Photograph: Dale Roddick

# CHAPTER 7

# INSTALLATION, CARE & USE

Y<small>ES, YOU</small> *CAN* <small>WALK</small> on a floorcloth! Properly cared for, it should last for decades. Today there are even a few centuries-old rugs still in existence (see the appendix, page 139), but unfortunately, most have succumbed to improper or lack of care and changing fashions. If you take good care of your rug by cleaning it regularly and handling it properly, it should serve you well for as long as you care to use it.

## INSTALLATION

Once your floorcloth is finished and ready for that special spot you planned it for, there are a few things you should know before you lay it in place. The relative thinness and flexibility of the painted canvas allow it to take on the characteristics of the surface beneath it, be it an uneven floor or errant dust bunny. For this reason, place your rug on as clean and flat a surface as possible.

First clean the floor well, vacuuming and then damp mopping to catch any particles of dirt that may be left behind. Then check the bottom of the floorcloth itself to be sure there aren't any foreign particles or bumpy spots on the rubber backing.

If the floorcloth has been rolled and is cold, give it a chance to warm up before unrolling it slowly and positioning it. (Large rugs with rubber backings may require two people to handle them.) When you're satisfied it's in the right place, give the rug time to relax and flatten out naturally. Do not force the floorcloth to unroll; as it warms to room temperature, it will return to its flat, flexible self and be ready for many years of use.

Consider what furniture will be placed on top of the rug and check for feet that could scratch it. If necessary, use a protective coaster under the leg or a plastic glide attached to the leg itself. These will protect the floorcloth surface as well as make the furniture easier to move around.

To avoid excessive wear in the same spot, you can rotate your floorcloth periodically if the design and location permit.

Previous page: Judith Barker-Schwartz, *Red Butler*, 8' x 11' (2.4 x 3.3 m), hand-painted and appliquéd acrylics
Photograph: Karen Mauch

Above: Rhonda Kaplan, *Dalmatians*, 2' x 3' (61 x 91.5 cm), hand-painted latex
Photograph: Jay Friedlander

## CLEANING

You will be pleasantly surprised at how easily your floorcloth cleans up. Even persistent blemishes, such as mustard stains and scuff marks, disappear.

The early directions for cleaning a floorcloth still hold true today. Soft soapy water, made with a mild dish detergent, and a damp sponge or mop are all that you need for regular care. Before you mop, eliminate excess dirt or grit by vacuuming the rug and the area around it well. Gently flip back the corners and vacuum underneath, as dirt has a way of sneaking under there.

After mopping the floorcloth with soapy water, rinse off any soapy residue and wipe the rug dry. Spots or particularly dirty areas can be safely cleaned with a small amount of mild liquid abrasive cleanser. Use cleanser sparingly and wipe it gently over the soiled area, being careful not to scrub too vigorously and mar the acrylic sealer. For dirt that is trapped in low spots, use a sponge or an old-fashioned scrub brush with soft bristles. Finally, rinse well and wipe dry.

*Warning: Avoid the following modern cleaners, which seem to cause problems with floorcloths: oil soaps (they leave a sticky residue); abrasive, gritty cleansers, except in liquid form; alcohol- and ammonia-based cleaners.*

Your floorcloth will last longer and be easier to maintain if you periodically renew the wax coating. Remove old wax by washing the rug with hot water and a mild liquid abrasive cleanser; then thoroughly clean and dry the rug and apply a thin coat of good-quality clear, nonyellowing paste wax. Allow the wax to dry before buffing it to a sheen with a soft cloth.

Top: Joyce Poynton, *Clothesline*, 4' x 8' (1.2 x 2.4 m), stenciled, hand-painted, and woodgrained acrylics and latex
Photograph: Evan Bracken

Bottom: S. Carter Keffury, *Sir Gawain*, 4' x 6' (1.2 x 1.8 m), hand-painted acrylics
Photograph: Scott Porter

*TAKE a Sponge or cloth, and wash them well with soft Water; then rub them quite dry with a clean Cloth — When very dirty, use a soft Scrubbing Brush and a lather of Soap; always wash the Soapy Water clean off, and rub them dry, as before directed.*

(From the scrapbook, *Manufactures & Arts of the 18 century* [sic], compiled by Robert Barnes, 1857, and preserved in the Victoria & Albert Museum, London)

There are just two things to avoid with your floorcloth: putting it in the washing machine or leaving it outdoors for extended periods!

## STORAGE

Although the best way to store a floorcloth is to leave it lying flat on the floor, sometimes rugs must be moved or stored. If you cannot store your rug flat (protected with a piece of soft fabric or clean paper), then you'll need to roll it on a rigid tube at least 4 to 6 inches (10 to 15 cm) in diameter. Plastic drainage pipe from a home-supply store makes an excellent tube that cannot be crushed. A larger-diameter tube minimizes surface stress, which can lead to cracking. Despite the flexibility of the canvas, folding a floorcloth can cause cracks in the painted surface or create stubborn creases.

Although opinions vary, there does not appear to be a noticeable difference between rolling a floorcloth with the design facing inside or outside—both approaches seem to work well. However, rolling the rug design-in protects the paint from being inadvertently damaged, and, when you go to unroll it again for use, the rug unrolls with the underside down and thus does not have to be flipped.

## REPAIR

If you follow the instructions in this book, you shouldn't experience many of the following problems, but sometimes, even with the best of care, a floorcloth can develop areas of wear or become damaged. Heavy use can show its effects on edges and spots where furniture has been moved around. Folding or bending can cause cracks. It may be easier and less expensive simply to replace a badly damaged rug, but most problems can be repaired.

**Worn areas** of a design can be touched up with the appropriate colors of paint. First clean the rug thoroughly, using a scrub brush and hot water to remove the wax, as paint products will not adhere to a waxed surface. If you don't have your original paints on hand, small amounts of artist's acrylics can be custom mixed to blend unobtrusively. Touch up the design as necessary. When the paint has dried, seal it with the same varnish used

*These carpets possess a decided advantage over all others, as they are more durable, and in warm weather much more comfortable, and easier to keep clean, and in hot climates the only kind that are not subject to injury from insects; in winter they may be covered with other carpeting without damage, and the room is kept warmer...*

(*New Hampshire Gazette*, April 8, 1828)

Opposite: Ben Jennings, *Garden Walk with Topiary Bushes*, 36' x 146' (11 x 44.5 m), hand-painted and sponged latex and acrylics

Top: Margaret Henkel, *My Dog Raul*, 28" x 35" (71 x 89 cm), hand-painted latex

Bottom: Tara Loughlin, *Oranges*, 7' x 9' (2.1 x 2.7 m), stippled and hand-painted oils
Photograph: Kevin Brusie

on the original rug, if it seems to need it; then apply a clear, nonyellowing wax.

If your floorcloth shows wear along the edges, dip a sponge in the appropriate color paint and rub it over the edges. After the paint has dried, reseal it.

**Cracking** or **crazing** of the painted surface can result from combining paint products that aren't chemically compatible: the various layers don't bond properly, and they expand and contract at different rates. The safest way to avoid this problem is to use primers, paints, and sealers from the same family of materials (i.e., all water based or oil based); this results in a marriage of layers that move together when subjected to the effects of heating, cooling, and aging.

A floorcloth that is cracked from folding should be allowed to flatten out naturally by being left on the floor in a warm room. If necessary, remove the wax; then touch up along the cracks with paint and sealer, as described above.

**Yellowing** is primarily a problem with oil-based varnishes and is most noticeable over white-painted areas. Unfortunately, once it occurs, there's not much that can be done about it except to enjoy the "antiqued" appearance. With acrylic sealers, yellowing shouldn't be a problem.

**Fading** doesn't seem to be a problem with most floorcloths, even though many of them are made for sun rooms. The light fastness of a particular paint depends on the chemical nature of the pigment; the heavier the pigment, the less apt it is to fade. If fading is a consideration, inquire about the paint's ultraviolet properties before you purchase it. In general, painted surfaces are more stable than dyed fabrics.

**Scratching** through everyday use is not a problem with floorcloths; rather, they seem to acquire a mellow patina as they age. Scratches in paint or sealer through abuse can be touched up as described above.

## SHIPPING

Although floorcloths can be stored loosely rolled around a tube, for shipping they require extra protection. Layer the floorcloth between clean unprinted paper or thin packing foam; then roll it around a rigid tube at least 6 inches (15 cm) in diameter. When you're finished rolling, tape securely around the outside of the paper or foam to hold everything in place around the tube. The rug will be safe whether rolled with the design facing in or out; however, by rolling the design in, it can be unrolled onto the floor without having to be flipped.

Kathy Cooper, *Absract Floral with Ribbons*, 9' x 12' (2.7 x 3.6 m), hand-painted acrylics
Photograph: Gary Warnimont

This is particularly advantageous with runners and large rugs, where flipping could inadvertently lead to folding, which might crease or crack the rug.

Ship the rolled rug inside another tube or a box. The outer container should closely match the dimensions of the rolled piece in order to prevent unnecessary movement of the rug. Boxes from fluorescent light tubes and the corrugated tubes that are used as cement forms are both handy for shipping smaller rugs.

A very large canvas may need to be shipped by freight. For freight shipment, roll the floorcloth onto a tube and pack it within a larger plastic pipe. Tape the ends securely. The package is likely to be transported on a forklift, so take the time to pack it well.

Top: Susan Kee, *Purple Vanity*, 5' x 6' (1.5 x 1.8 m), stenciled, dry-brushed, ragged, and sponged latex and acrylics with textured overlays
Photograph: Dale Roddick

Bottom: Shari Cornish, *Househeads #2*, 58" x 72" (1.5 x 1.8 m), silk-screened fabric pigment on industrial felt
Photograph: B. Miller

# LOCATIONS OF HISTORIC FLOORCLOTHS

The following historic properties have original or reproduction floorcloths in their collections; some are not on display but may be seen by appointment.

Thomas Stocker, *Turkish Prayer Rug* (19th century), 43" x 53" (1 x 1.3 m), hand-painted and stenciled acrylics
Photograph: Eric Davis

## UNITED STATES

### CONNECTICUT

Darien Historical Society
Darien, CT
(203) 655-9233

Webb-Deane-Stevens Museum
Silas Deane House
Wethersfield, CT
(860) 529-0612

### DELAWARE

Buena Vista
Delaware State Museums
Dover, DE
(302) 739-5316

Henry Francis du Pont Winterthur
Museum
Winterthur, DE
(302) 888-4600

### DISTRICT OF COLUMBIA

Daughters of the American
Revolution Museum
Washington, DC
(202) 879-3241

### GEORGIA

Hardaway House
Thomasville Landmarks
Thomasville, GA
(912) 226-6016

Owens Thomas House
Savannah, GA
(912) 233-9743

### ILLINOIS

Lincoln Homestead
Springfield, IL
(217) 492-4241

### MASSACHUSETTS

Elias Derby House
Salem, MA
(508) 744-4323

Essex Institute
Gardner-Pingree House and
Andrew Safford House
Salem, MA
(508) 745-1876

Old Sturbridge Village
Sturbridge, MA
(508) 347-3362

Salisbury Mansion
Worcester Historical Museum
Worcester, MA
(508) 753-8278

### MICHIGAN

Greenfield Village
Dearborn, MI
(313) 271-1620

### MINNESOTA

Oliver H. Kelley Farm
Minnesota Historical Society
Elk River, MN
(612) 441-6896

### MISSISSIPPI

Natchez National Historic Park
Melrose Plantation
Natchez, MI
(601) 446-5790

### NEW YORK

Boscobel
Garrison, NY
(914) 265-3638

Brooklyn Museum
Brooklyn, NY
(718) 638-5000

New York State Historical
Association
Cooperstown, NY
(607) 547-1400

Silas Wright House
St. Lawrence County Historic
Association
Canton, NY
(315) 386-8133

Joseph Lloyd Manor
Huntington, NY
(516) 271-7760

Women's Rights National Historic
Park
Elizabeth Cady Stanton House
Seneca Falls, NY
(315) 568-2991

Thompson House
Setauket, NY
(516) 941-9444

## NORTH CAROLINA

Hope Plantation
Windsor, NC
(919) 794-3140

Museum of Early Southern
Decorative Arts
Winston-Salem, NC
(910) 721-7360

## TENNESSEE

The Hermitage
Nashville, TN
(615) 889-2941

Rock Castle
Hendersonville, TN
(615) 824-0502

## VIRGINIA

The Carlyle House
Alexandria, VA
(703) 549-2997

Colonial Williamsburg
Williamsburg, VA
(804) 229-1000

Magnolia Grange
Chesterfield, VA
(804) 748-1026

Point of Honor
Lynchburg, VA
(804) 847-1459

The White House of the Confederacy
Richmond, VA
(804) 649-1861

Wilton House Museum
Richmond, VA
(804) 282-5936

## CANADA

### ONTARIO

Fort York Historic Site
Toronto
(416) 392-6907

Royal Ontario Museum
Toronto
(416) 586-5549

The Museum of Textiles
Toronto
(416) 599-5321

Upper Canada Village
Morrisburg
(613) 543-3704

### QUEBEC

Canadian Museum of Civilization
Hull
(819) 776-8364

## GREAT BRITAIN

Belton House
Grantham, Lincolnshire
01476 566116

The Bowes Museum
Barnard Castle, Durham
01833 690606

Calke Abbey
Ticknall, Derbyshire
01332 863822

Temple Newsam House
Leeds, West Yorkshire
01132 647321

Maryellen Murphy, *Hooked Rugs, Oak Leaves*, 22" x 96" (.5 x 2.4 m), hand-painted acrylics with rug fringe
Photograph: Kate Cameron

# PARTICIPATING ARTISTS

CRISTINA ACOSTA
Bend, Oregon

HEATHER J. ALLEN
Asheville, NC

MARJORIE A. ATWOOD
Tulsa, OK

STUART BAILEY
Richmond, VA

JOYCE BARKER-SCHWARTZ
Barker-Schwartz Designs
Philadelphia, PA

BARBARA P. BENSON
The Bensons Fiber & Wood, Etc.
Camden, ME

SUE BLEYAERT
Creative Canvas
Petosky, MI

PAT BURGEE
Tapetto Marmo
Baltimore, MD

LIZ CHASE
Chicago, IL

KATHY COOPER
Orchard House Floorcloths
King, NC

SHARI CORNISH
St. Paul, MN

LAURA CURRAN
Fun Fibers
Northampton, MA

MALEESA DAVIS
Footprints
Denver, CO

PATRICIA DREHER
Berkeley, CA

JEAN EBERT
Jean Ebert Decorative Painting
Winston-Salem, NC

Margaret Henkel, *Rooster at Dawn*, 29" x 40" (73.5 x 101.5 cm), hand-painted latex

ELLIE ERNST
Ernst Designs
Montgomery, AL

EVERGREENE PAINTING STUDIOS
New York, NY

KIKI FARISH
Artysseys
Smithfield, NC

BARBARA FARRELL
barbara farrell ARTS
Sanford, FL

BRIGID FINUCANE
Chicago, IL

MARCI FORBES
Cleveland, OH

LAURA GARDNER
Charlotte, NC

CHARLES GOFORTH
Fayetteville, NC

SUE HARDY
Sue Hardy Originals
Jonesboro, AR

JAN HARRIS
Butner, NC

MARGARET HENKEL
Margaret Henkel Folk Artist
Shrewsbury, VT

DEEDA HULL
Deeda Designs
Takoma Park, MD

BEN JENNINGS
Ben Jennings Designs
Atlanta, GA

RHONDA KAPLAN
East Lake Designs
Annapolis, MD

SUSAN KEE
Toronto, Ontario, Canada

**S. CARTER KEFFURY**
Lemonheads
Berkeley, CA

**VIRGINIA KIRSCH**
Virginia Kirsch
Floorcloths
San Francisco, CA

**HILARY LAW**
Boston, MA

**SHARON D. LEE**
The Painted House
Philadelphia, PA

**TARA LOUGHLIN**
Loughlin Studio
Portland, ME

**GARY MACKENDER**
Tucson, AZ

**PAMELA MARWEDE**
Longboat Key, FL

**CAROL MASSENBURG**
Artysseys
Smithfield, NC

**BILLY MCCLAIN**
Winston-Salem, NC

**CALLAHAN K. MCDONOUGH**
Atlanta, GA

**CONSTANCE MILLER**
Spiritcloth
Bainbridge Island, WA

**MARY MOROSS**
Mary Moross Studios
New York, NY

**ROGER MUDRE**
Roger Mudre
Decorative Painting
Weston, CT

**MARYELLEN MURPHY**
M. E. Murphy Designs
Berkeley, CA

**ANGIE NELSON**
Homeplace Collection
Thomasville, NC

**MAUREEN O'DONNELL**
Colonial Floorcloths
Catonsville, MD

**SUSAN PAPA**
Midlothian, VA

**JOYCE POYNTON**
Raleigh, NC

**FRANCIE ANNE RILEY**
Riley Design
Shenorock, NY

**SUSAN ROBERTSON**
Painted Turtle Productions
Roslindale, MA

**LAURA M. ROGERS**
First State Fancies
Newark, DE

**GABRIEL ROMEU**
Philadelphia, PA

**FRAN RUBINSTEIN**
Divine Inspirations
Grafton, WI

**PAT SCHEIBLE**
Pat Scheible Painting
Specialties
Mebane, NC

**BRENDA SHANNON**
Winter Hill Studio
Franconia, NH

**POMONA SHEA**
Surry, ME

**GEORGE W. SHINN**
Canvas Carpet Company
Philadelphia, PA

**CARMON SLATER**
Winds Reach Designs
Evergreen, CO

**GINNY A. SPEIRS**
Truly Trompe
Winston-Salem, NC

**THOMAS J. STOCKER**
Boston, MA

**LAURINDA STOCKWELL**
Jersey City, NJ

**REBECCA SYKES**
Fresco Studio
Burlington, VT

**MARY VAN VLIET**
Olive Design
Brooklyn, NY

**ALAN VAUGHN**
Alan Vaughn Studios
Atlanta, GA

**SUSAN J. WARLICK**
Artifects
Raleigh, NC

**JOAN WEISSMAN**
Custom Rugs & Tapestries
Albuquerque, NM

Constance Miller, *Wavy Green Runner*, 30" x 72" (.8 x 1.8 m), felt-stamped acrylics
Photograph: Michael Seidl

# ACKNOWLEDGMENTS

No book grows full-blown out of an author's head; rather, it blossoms with assistance and sustenance from many directions. It isn't possible here to thank all those who suggested, supported, aided, and abetted, but there are a few who must be named.

First of all, thank you to Toni Sikes, editor of *The Guild*, who encouraged us and helped start our list of artists' names. This book owes its depth to the more than 100 artists who responded to our artist search and took the time to fill out our six-page questionnaire and share their experience and heretofore proprietary technical information. Along with their art, philosophies, and enthusiasm, these artists are helping to finally answer the recurring question, "Can you walk on them?"

We are particularly grateful to the artists who contributed decorative techniques or designed projects (or both): Joyce Barker-Schwartz, Barbara Benson, Pat Burgee, Kiki Farish, Sue Hardy, Ben Jennings, Rhonda Kaplan, Virginia Kirsch, Sharon Lee, Billy McClain, Mary Moross, Maryellen Murphy, Francie Riley, Pat Scheible, Pomona Shea, George Shinn, and Laurinda Stockwell. Thanks also to Laura Curran, Constance Miller, and Susan Warlick, who provided invaluable technical information.

Another 90-plus artists contributed photos for this book. Though every image could not be included, the tremendous variety of work gave life to the project. The Museum of Early Southern Decorative Arts, especially Director of Research Brad Rauschenburg and Research Associate Martha Rowe, supported us during many stages of this work; Susan Gonzalez made numerous trips to the Victoria and Albert Museum and photographed the Barnes scrapbook for our research; Karen Hersey gave of her legal expertise; Cappy Kuhn added a professional look to our original questionnaire; and artists Nancy Cayford, Mari Elin Chamney, Brigid Finucane, and Virginia Kirsch generously shared their own research materials.

For technical support, special thanks to Stokes Paints and Tina at TenPlus. And for another kind of technical support, sincere appreciation for the patience and insights of our Lark Books publisher, Rob Pulleyn, editor, Leslie Dierks, and designer, Kathy Holmes.

And finally, there are our families, who managed without Mom more than they would have liked—Tom, Sunny, and Libba Cooper, and David, Page, and Tyler Hersey.

And yes, you can walk on them!

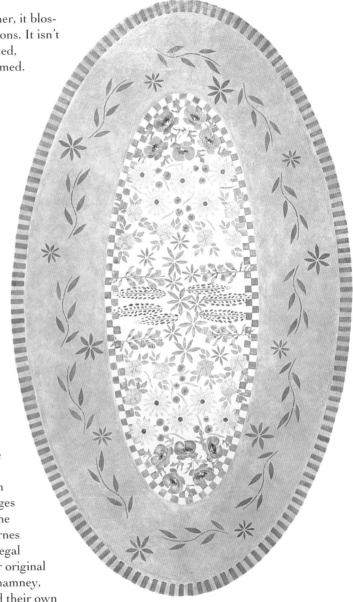

Brenda Shannon, *Flower Garden*, 4' x 7' (1.2 x 2.1 m), glazed, stenciled, and hand-painted acrylics
Photograph: Tom Long

**If you cannot find any of the tools and materials used in this book in your local craft and art supply stores, you can write for a partial list of mail-order suppliers. Send a business SASE to Lark Books, Attn. Ed. Asst., 50 College St., Asheville, NC 28801. Ask for the floor-cloth suppliers list.**

# INDEX

Alan Vaughn, *Hop Scotch*, 3' x 7' (.9 x 2.1 m), hand-painted acrylics with oil crayon